T IT

FIX IT

TE

DON'T JUST TEST IT, FIX IT!

English **Verbs and Tenses**

Kenna Bourke

OXFORD

UNIVERSITY PRESS

UNIVERSITY PRESS

Great Clarendon Street, Oxford OX2 6DP

Oxford University Press is a department of the University of Oxford.
It furthers the University's objective of excellence in research,
scholarship, and education by publishing worldwide in

Oxford New York

Auckland Bangkok Buenos Aires Cape Town Chennai
Dar es Salaam Delhi Hong Kong Istanbul Karachi Kolkata
Kuala Lumpur Madrid Melbourne Mexico City Mumbai Nairobi
São Paulo Shanghai Taipei Tokyo Toronto

Oxford and Oxford English are registered trade marks of
Oxford University Press in the UK and in certain other countries

ISBN 0 19 438074 2

Illustrated by Tamsin Cook

Text layout and design by
Cambridge Publishing Management Ltd

Printed in China

Contents

How to use *Test it, Fix it*

Test it, Fix it is a series of books designed to help you identify any problems you may have in English, and to fix the problems. Each *Test it, Fix it* book has twenty tests which concentrate on mistakes commonly made by learners.

Test it, Fix it has an unusual format. You start at the **first** page of each unit, then go to the **third** page, then to the **second** page. Here's how it works:

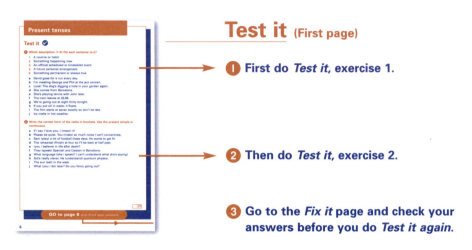

Test it (First page)

1 First do *Test it*, exercise 1.

2 Then do *Test it*, exercise 2.

3 Go to the *Fix it* page and check your answers before you do *Test it again*.

Fix it (Third page)

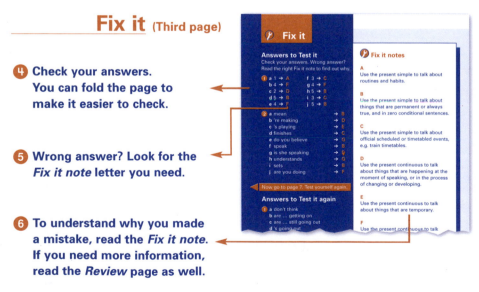

4 Check your answers. You can fold the page to make it easier to check.

5 Wrong answer? Look for the *Fix it note* letter you need.

6 To understand why you made a mistake, read the *Fix it note*. If you need more information, read the *Review* page as well.

7 Now go back to the second page and do *Test it again*.

Test it again (Second page)

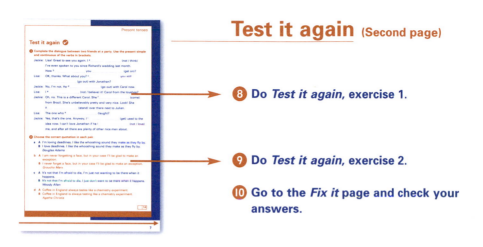

8 Do *Test it again*, exercise 1.

9 Do *Test it again*, exercise 2.

10 Go to the *Fix it* page and check your answers.

Fix it (Third page)

11 Check your answers.

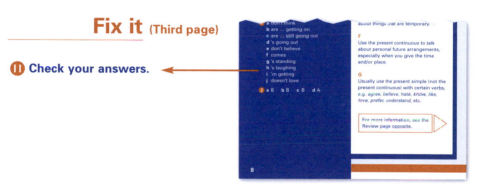

Review (Fourth page)

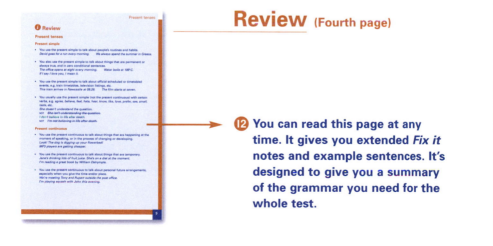

12 You can read this page at any time. It gives you extended *Fix it* notes and example sentences. It's designed to give you a summary of the grammar you need for the whole test.

Present tenses

Test it ✔

1 **Which description (1–5) fits each sentence (a–j)?**

1 A routine or habit
2 Something happening now
3 An official scheduled or timetabled event
4 A future personal arrangement
5 Something permanent or always true

a David goes for a run every day.
b I'm meeting George and Phil at the jazz concert.
c Look! The dog's digging a hole in your garden again.
d She comes from Barcelona.
e She's playing tennis with John later.
f The train leaves at 20.08.
g We're going out at eight thirty tonight.
h If you put oil in water, it floats.
i The film starts at seven exactly so don't be late.
j Ice melts in hot weather.

2 **Write the correct form of the verbs in brackets. Use the present simple or continuous.**

a If I say I love you, I (mean) it!
b Please be quiet. You (make) so much noise I can't concentrate.
c Sam (play) a lot of football these days. He wants to get fit.
d The rehearsal (finish) at four so I'll be back at half past.
e (you / believe) in life after death?
f They (speak) Spanish and Catalan in Barcelona.
g What language (she / speak)? I can't understand what she's saying!
h Sid's really clever. He (understand) quantum physics.
i The sun (set) in the west.
j What (you / do) later? Do you fancy going out?

20

GO to page 8 and check your answers.

Test it again ✔

❶ Complete the dialogue between two friends at a party. Use the present simple and continuous forms of the verbs in brackets.

Jackie: Lisa! Great to see you again. I ^a.................................... (not / think)

I've even spoken to you since Richard's wedding last month.

How ^b........................... you .... (get on)?

Lisa: OK, thanks. What about you? ^c.................................... you still

.... (go out) with Jonathan?

Jackie: No, I'm not. He ^d.................................... (go out) with Carol now.

Lisa: I ^e.................................... (not / believe) it! Carol from the toyshop?

Jackie: Oh, no. This is a different Carol. She ^f.................................... (come)

from Brazil. She's unbelievably pretty and very nice. Look! She

^g.................................... (stand) over there next to Julian.

Lisa: The one who ^h.................................... (laugh)?

Jackie: Yes, that's the one. Anyway, I ⁱ.................................... (get) used to the

idea now. I can't love Jonathan if he ^j.................................... (not / love)

me, and after all there are plenty of other nice men about.

❷ Choose the correct quotation in each pair.

a   **A** I'm loving deadlines. I like the whooshing sound they make as they fly by.
    B I love deadlines. I like the whooshing sound they make as they fly by.
    Douglas Adams

b   **A** I am never forgetting a face, but in your case I'll be glad to make an exception.
    B I never forget a face, but in your case I'll be glad to make an exception.
    Groucho Marx

c   **A** It's not that I'm afraid to die, I'm just not wanting to be there when it happens.
    B It's not that I'm afraid to die, I just don't want to be there when it happens.
    Woody Allen

d   **A** Coffee in England always tastes like a chemistry experiment.
    B Coffee in England is always tasting like a chemistry experiment.
    Agatha Christie

| 14 |

Fix it

Answers to Test it

Check your answers. Wrong answer?
Read the right Fix it note to find out why.

1
a 1 → A		f 3 → C		
b 4 → F		g 4 → F		
c 2 → D		h 5 → B		
d 5 → B		i 3 → C		
e 4 → F		j 5 → B		

2
a mean	→	B
b 're making	→	D
c 's playing	→	E
d finishes	→	C
e do you believe	→	G
f speak	→	B
g is she speaking	→	D
h understands	→	G
i sets	→	B
j are you doing	→	F

Now go to page 7. Test yourself again.

Answers to Test it again

1
a don't think
b are ... getting on
c are ... going out
d 's going out
e don't believe
f comes
g 's standing
h 's laughing
i 'm getting
j doesn't love

2 a B   b B   c B   d A

Fix it notes

A
Use the present simple to talk about routines and habits.

B
Use the present simple to talk about things that are permanent or always true, and in zero conditional sentences.

C
Use the present simple to talk about official scheduled or timetabled events, e.g. train timetables.

D
Use the present continuous to talk about things that are happening at the moment of speaking, or in the process of changing or developing.

E
Use the present continuous to talk about things that are temporary.

F
Use the present continuous to talk about personal future arrangements, especially when you give the time and/or place.

G
Usually use the present simple (not the present continuous) with certain verbs, e.g. *agree, believe, hate, know, like, love, prefer, understand*, etc.

For more information, see the Review page opposite.

ⓘ Review

Present tenses

Present simple

- You use the present simple to talk about people's routines and habits.
  David goes for a run every morning.   *We always spend the summer in Greece.*

- You also use the present simple to talk about things that are permanent or always true, and in zero conditional sentences.
  The office opens at eight every morning.   *Water boils at 100°C.*
  If I say I love you, I mean it.

- You use the present simple to talk about official scheduled or timetabled events, e.g. train timetables, television listings, etc.
  This train arrives in Newcastle at 08.28.   *The film starts at seven.*

- You usually use the present simple (not the present continuous) with certain verbs, e.g. *agree, believe, feel, hate, hear, know, like, love, prefer, see, smell, taste*, etc.
  She doesn't understand the question.
  NOT   *She isn't understanding the question.*
  I don't believe in life after death.
  NOT   *I'm not believing in life after death.*

Present continuous

- You use the present continuous to talk about things that are happening at the moment of speaking, or in the process of changing or developing.
  Look! The dog is digging up your flowerbed!
  MP3 players are getting cheaper.

- You use the present continuous to talk about things that are temporary.
  Jane's drinking lots of fruit juice. She's on a diet at the moment.
  I'm reading a great book by William Dalrymple.

- You use the present continuous to talk about personal future arrangements, especially when you give the time and/or place.
  We're meeting Tony and Rupert outside the post office.
  I'm playing squash with John this evening.

Used to, would, be used to, get used to

Test it ✅

1 Find and correct the mistake in each sentence.

a When I was a child, I didn't used to believe in Father Christmas.

f We'd often to go to look for shells on the beach.

b Would you have long hair when you were younger?

g Do you use to play any sports when you were at school?

c Did you used to watch a lot of TV?

h My brother used to frightening me with horrible spiders.

d I usedn't to like classical music but I love it now.

i Francis would always know he'd be famous one day.

e Are you getting used to live in the city now you've moved?

j Don't worry about the noise. I used to it.

2 Choose the best option.

When I was a boy, I ᵃ used to be/was being crazy about football.
I ᵇ would want/wanted to go to every match — in fact I even started my own football team. I ᶜ would be/was the captain, of course, and my friend, Harry, was the goalie because he was taller than I was. We ᵈ didn't/wouldn't have many players but there were a few. Harry ᵉ use to/used to believe that one day we'd both be professional football players but of course that never happened.

15

GO to page 12 and check your answers.

Test it again ✔

1 Choose the correct option, **A** or **B**.

a   .... have blonde hair?
   A Didn't you use to   **B** Are you used to

b   When I was a teenager, I .... watch TV all the time.
   A was used to   **B** used to

c   Pete soon .... travelling between home and work.
   A got used to   **B** used to

d   .... living in the country after living in New York?
   A Did you use to   **B** Are you getting used to

e   As a child, she .... dream of living in a castle.
   A would   **B** is used to

f   I .... getting up early so I didn't mind starting work at seven.
   A used to   **B** was used to

g   We .... eat fish but now we have it two or three times a week.
   A weren't used to   **B** never used to

h   Dad .... get a lot of headaches. Now he doesn't.
   A was used to   **B** used to

i   Do you think we .... living in London?
   A 'll get used to   **B** used to

j   The children .... often play hide-and-seek in the woods.
   A got used to   **B** would

k   My sister .... be a teacher. Now she's a painter.
   A got used to   **B** used to

2 Choose the best caption for the cartoon.

We would think it was unusual but we're getting used to it now.
We used to think it was unusual but we were used to it now.
We used to think it was unusual but we're getting used to it now.

12

🔧 Fix it

Answers to Test it

Check your answers. Wrong answer?
Read the right Fix it note to find out why.

1
a	~~used~~	use	→ **B**
b	~~Would you~~		
	Did you/Did you use to		→ **F**
c	~~used~~	use	→ **C**
d	~~usedn't to~~		
	didn't use to/used not to		→ **B**
e	~~live~~	living	→ **H**
f	~~to go~~	go	→ **E**
g	~~Do~~	Did	→ **C, D**
h	~~frightening~~ frighten		→ **A**
i	~~would ... know~~		
	used to know/		
	(always) knew		→ **F**
j	~~used~~	am used	→ **G**

2
a	used to be	→ **D**
b	wanted	→ **F**
c	was	→ **F**
d	didn't	→ **F**
e	used to	→ **A**

◄ Now go to page 11. Test yourself again.

Answers to Test it again

1
a A	**b** B	**c** A	**d** B
e A	**f** B	**g** B	**h** B
i A	**j** B	**k** B	

2 We used to think it was unusual
but we're getting used to it now.

🔧 Fix it notes

A
Form the affirmative of *used to* with
subject + *used to* + base form of the verb.

B
Form the negative of *used to* with
subject + *didn't use to* + base form. You
can also use subject + *used not to* or
never used to + base form of the verb.

C
Form the interrogative of *used to* with
did + subject + *use to* + base form of
the verb.

D
Use *used to* for things that happened
in the past but don't happen now.

E
Use *would* + base form of the verb.
Don't use the infinitive or an *-ing* form.

F
Use *would* for past repeated actions
or habits. Don't use *would* with state
verbs.

G
Use *be used to* + noun or *-ing* form
to say that someone or something is
familiar to you.

H
Use *get used to* + noun or *-ing* form
to say that someone or something is
becoming familiar to you.

For more information, see the
Review page opposite. ▷

 Review

Used to, would, be used to, get used to

Used to

- You form the affirmative of *used to* with subject + *used to* + base form of the verb. Don't use the infinitive or an *-ing* form.
  We used to live in Brussels.   NOT   ~~We used to to live in Brussels.~~
  ~~We used to living in Brussels.~~

- You form the negative with subject + *didn't use to* + base form of the verb. You can also use subject + *used not to* or *never used to* + base verb. Don't use *usedn't to*.
  I didn't use to like coffee.   OR   *I used not to like/I never used to like coffee.*
  NOT   ~~I usedn't to like coffee.~~

- You form the interrogative with *did* + subject + *use to* + base form of the verb.
  Did you use to have long hair?

- You use *used to* for things that happened in the past but don't happen now.
  I used to smoke.   *Pete used to play the piano.*
  (But I don't now.)   (But he doesn't any more.)

Would

- You use *would* + base form of the verb. Don't use the infinitive or an *-ing* form.
  The children would collect stones and shells on the beach every summer.
  NOT   ~~The children would to collect…~~   ~~The children would collecting…~~

- You use *would* for past repeated actions or habits. Don't use *would* with state verbs. Use the past simple or *used to* instead.
  I would often go to see my old history teacher.
  NOT   ~~I would have long hair…~~   ~~We would know each other well…~~

Be/get used to

- You use *be used to* to say that someone or something is familiar to you. You can use *be used to* in the present and the past. Use a noun or an *-ing* form after *be used to*.
  I'm used to getting up early in the morning. (I do it often.)
  I was used to working long hours in my last job. (I often worked long hours.)

- You use *get used to* to say that someone or something is becoming familiar to you. You can use *get used to* with all tenses. Use a noun or an *-ing* form after *get used to*.
  I got used to life on the farm.   *I'm getting used to living here.*
  (It became familiar to me.)   (I'm becoming accustomed to it.)

Present perfect or past simple?

Test it ✔

1 Find and correct the mistake in each sentence.

a Didn't you do your homework yet?

b Pete's been to the shops. He'll be back soon.

c Did you ever eat snails?

d We're here since ten o'clock.

e No one's seen Lucky since three weeks.

f I had a headache since I woke up this morning.

g Have you called John yesterday?

h A plane just crashed over the Alps. More details follow later.

i When I was a child, I have ridden my bike to school.

j I have never met my grandmother. She died before I was born.

2 Match the statements.

5 **a** Oh, no! I've just smashed a glass.
7 **b** I've already written fifteen emails.
9 **c** Did you go to Teotihuacan while you were in Mexico?
10 **d** I worked here last year.
1 **e** Sam's gone out.
2 **f** I read five reports at work today.
6 **g** I've worked here since 1999.
8 **h** I smashed a glass. I didn't mean to.
3 **i** Have you ever been to Teotihuacan?
4 **j** Sam's been out.

1 Sam's not here.
2 I'm not at the office.
3 I'm asking about your general experience of travelling.
4 Sam's here.
5 Look. The glass is broken.
6 I still work here.
7 I'm still at the office.
8 I smashed it yesterday.
9 I'm asking about your holiday.
10 Now I work somewhere else.

20

GO to page 16 and check your answers.

Test it again ✓

1 Choose the best option.

a Jim's never seen/never saw this film. I'm sure he'll like it.

b Wow! Did you already do/Have you already done the housework?

c They didn't get/haven't got married in the end.

d I haven't been on holiday for/since ages.

e Frances has been/gone to Jamaica. She'll be back next month.

f I live/I've lived here for eight years.

g The rabbit dug/has dug a hole in our garden last night.

h A tornado has hit/hit north-west America and several people were killed.

i Hey look! Concorde's just landed/just landed.

j Ever since I was a child I wanted/I've wanted to go to Zanzibar.

2 Which description (1–4) fits each sentence (a–j)?

1 A recent action in the past with an effect in the present

2 A finished action in the past

3 An action which started in the past and is still going on now

4 A past action at an indefinite time in the past

a I've never been to Tibet.

b Stan has had that car for years.

c We took the dog to the vet's yesterday.

d I've finished my homework at last.

e Pete's just finished painting the kitchen.

f We had oysters and champagne last night.

g They've known each other since they were kids.

h Rick's been to Malaysia several times.

i Didn't you see David last week?

j Mireia's just had a baby girl.

20

Fix it

Answers to Test it

Check your answers. Wrong answer?
Read the right Fix it note to find out why.

1
a ~~Didn't you do~~
  Haven't you done   → **D**
b ~~been~~   gone   → **C**
c ~~Did you ever eat~~
  Have you ever eaten   → **B**
d ~~'re~~   've been   → **E**
e ~~since~~   for   → **F**
f ~~had~~   've had   → **E**
g ~~Have you called~~
  Did you call   → **A**
h ~~crashed~~
  has just crashed   → **D**
i ~~have ridden~~ rode   → **A**
j ~~have never met~~
  never met   → **A**

2
a 5 → **D**   f 2 → **A**
b 7 → **E**   g 6 → **E**
c 9 → **A**   h 8 → **A**
d 10 → **A**   i 3 → **B**
e 1 → **C**   j 4 → **C**

Now go to page 15. Test yourself again.

Answers to Test it again

1
a 's never seen
b Have you already done
c didn't get
d for
e gone
f I've lived
g dug
h hit
i 's just landed
j I've wanted

2
a 4   b 3   c 2   d 1   e 1
f 2   g 3   h 4   i 2   j 1

Fix it notes

A
Use the past simple for completed actions in the past.

B
Use the present perfect (not the past simple) when it isn't important when something happened.

C
There is a difference between the participles *been* and *gone*.

D
Use the present perfect (not the past simple) to talk about recent past events.

E
Use the present perfect (not the past simple or the present simple) to talk about an action that began in the past but is still going on now.

F
Use *for* (not *since*) with the present perfect to say how long an action has been going on.

For more information, see the Review page opposite.

 Review

Present perfect or past simple?

The difference between the past simple and the present perfect causes problems for many people. This is perhaps partly because there are several ways of using the present perfect. Here are some guidelines to help you decide which tense to use.

Past simple

- You use the past simple for completed actions in the past, often with an expression of time, e.g. *yesterday, last week, in 2001, a few years ago*, etc.
  We took the dog to the vet's yesterday.
  I went to South Africa when I was a student.

Present perfect

- You use the present perfect (not the past simple) when it isn't important when something happened. Often you're talking about general experiences.
  I've never been to a safari park before.   *Have you seen this film?*

- Be careful! There is a difference between the participles *been* and *gone*.
  Jill has been to Zanzibar.   *Jill has gone to Zanzibar.*
  (She went to Zanzibar and now she's back.)   (She's in Zanzibar now.)

- You use the present perfect (not the past simple) to talk about recent past events, often with *just, already* and *yet*.
  I've just seen Matt.   *We've already told him.*   *Haven't you finished that yet?*

   Note: In American English, it's possible to use either the present perfect or the past simple with the adverbs *just, already* and *yet*. Both are correct.
  Haven't you finished that yet?   OR   *Didn't you finish that yet?*

- You use the present perfect (not the past simple or the present simple) to talk about an action that began in the past but is still going on now.
  I've lived in Oxford for years.   *She's had that car since she was seventeen.*

Note: You use *for* to say how long an action has been going on and *since* to say when the action started.
*I've been here **for** ages.*   *She's known him **since** last year.*
*They've lived in Siena **for** three years.* *He's had a cold **since** Friday.*

Present perfect simple or present perfect continuous?

Test it ✔

1 Choose the best captions for the cartoons.

a He's been working all night.
He's worked all night.

b I've always been knowing the dog was strange.
I've always known the dog was strange.

2 Choose the best option.

a At last! I've solved/been solving the problem.
b Jack has been trying/tried to get his book published for ages but so far no one has said 'Yes'.
c So, what have you done/been doing recently? Anything interesting?
d My friend has been buying/bought a new car. It looks great.
e I've never believed/been believing in ghosts or witches or fairies.
f Fantastic news! They've been agreeing/agreed to buy the house!
g You look well. Have you been taking/taken more exercise recently?
h The children are tired because they've played/been playing all day.
i Have you swum/been swimming? Your hair looks wet.
j Oh, there you are! I've looked/been looking for you everywhere!

12

GO to page 20 and check your answers.

Present perfect simple or present perfect continuous?

Test it again ✔

1 **Find the correct sentence in each pair.**

a You're wet! What have you been doing?
b You're wet! What have you done?

c I've never understood maths.
d I've never been understanding maths.

e He's tired because he's run.
f He's tired because he's been running.

g I've been walking ten kilometres!
h I've walked ten kilometres!

i Sorry I'm late. How long have you waited?
j Sorry I'm late. How long have you been waiting?

2 **Complete the dialogue. Use the correct form of the verbs in brackets. If two forms are possible, write both.**

Sarah: Wow, it ª .... (be) very busy in the shop this morning, hasn't it?

Kim: Yes. I ᵇ .... (put) new stock on the shelves since I got here. There ᶜ .... (not / be) a quiet period at all. The phone in the office ᵈ .... (ring) every two minutes, so I ᵉ .... (answer) that and I ᶠ .... (try) to answer all the emails that the customer services department ᵍ .... (send) me!

Sarah: Yes, I know how you feel. It's incredible! I ʰ .... (write) replies to twenty emails. And I ⁱ .... (serve) all the customers that ʲ .... (come) in today.

15

Fix it

Answers to Test it

Check your answers. Wrong answer?
Read the right Fix it note to find out why.

1 **a** He's been working all
    night.   → **A**
  b I've always known the
    dog was strange.   → **C**

2 **a** solved   → **B**
  b been trying   → **A**
  c been doing   → **A**
  d bought   → **B**
  e believed   → **C**
  f agreed   → **C**
  g been taking   → **A**
  h been playing   → **A**
  i been swimming → **A**
  j been looking   → **A**

Now go to page 19. Test yourself again.

Answers to Test it again

1 The correct sentences are:
  a   **c**   **f**   **h**   **j**

2 **a** has been
  b 've been putting
  c hasn't been
  d has been ringing
  e 've been answering
  f 've been trying
  g have been sending/have sent
  h 've written
  i 've been serving/'ve served
  j have come

 **Fix it notes**

A

Use the present perfect continuous
when the activity is important, or is still
happening now.

B

Use the present perfect simple when
the result of a completed activity is
important.

C

Use the present perfect simple (not the
present perfect continuous) with verbs
that are not usually used in the
continuous form, e.g. *agree, believe,
know,* etc.

For more information, see the
Review page opposite.

 # Review

Present perfect simple or present perfect continuous?

Present perfect simple	Present perfect continuous
I've done all my work!	I've been doing a report on the sales figures.
She's run the London marathon twice.	She's been running – she looks tired!
Have they revised for tomorrow's exam?	Have they been revising or not?

It can be difficult to know whether the simple or continuous form is the correct one when you're using the present perfect. Sometimes there isn't much difference and it won't matter which you choose. However, there are two things you can consider when you're deciding between the two.

- You use the present perfect continuous when the activity that you're talking about is important. The activity may have finished recently or it may still be going on.
  He's been running for two hours already.
  (And he's still running now.)
  They've been painting the ceiling.
  (That explains why they have paint on their clothes.)

- You use the present perfect simple when you feel that the result of a completed activity is important.
  He's run the marathon.
  (This is an important achievement.)
  They've painted the ceiling.
  (The result is important. It looks better now.)

Note: Quite often it doesn't matter whether you use the simple form or the continuous. The meaning is the same or very similar.
Jim's worked all night.   *I've had a bad dream.*
Jim's been working all night.   *I've been having a bad dream.*

However, use the present perfect simple (not the present perfect continuous) with verbs that are not usually used in the continuous form, e.g. *agree, believe, know,* etc.
I've known Pete for a long time.   NOT   *I've been knowing Pete for a long time.*

Since, for and ago

Test it ✅

1 **Find the incorrect sentences.**

a This is the first time I ate crab.

b No one has been in this house for years.

c Harry and Sally have known each other since two weeks.

d I've been to Egypt nearly twenty years ago.

e It's two years since my rabbit has died.

f He's been working here since three months.

g Hey! Watch out! That's the third time you trod on my toe.

h Pete and Katy met at the school reunion. They hadn't spoken to each other since 1990.

i We've been in love with each other for years and years.

j Ten years ago, an old woman lived here with her three cats.

2 **Complete the sentences. Use *ago, for* or *since*.**

a Mike's had that old car .... eight years.

b I last spoke to Tim two weeks ....

c 'How long have you been waiting?' '................................... half-past two.'

d I've felt much better .... I started going for walks.

e That film was made over twenty years ....

f This is the first time I've seen you .... the wedding.

g Nick has been working .... hours. He must be tired.

h Have you put on weight .... you stopped smoking?

i No one's seen Simon .... three weeks.

j I went to the Sinai many years .... , when I was still a student.

20

GO to page 24 and check your answers.

22

Test it again ✔

❶ Answer the questions. Use *for* or *since* and the words in brackets.

   a How long have you been seeing Jason? (two months)
   b How long have you owned your flat? (1999)
   c How long have they been here? (a couple of days)
   d How long has John been working there? (two years)
   e How long have they been on holiday? (last Saturday)
   f How long has the shop been open? (nine o'clock)
   g How long have you been waiting? (an hour)
   h How long have you been studying English? (last autumn)
   i How long has he had his dog? (September)
   j How long have you known Tony? (Christmas)

❷ Write the correct form of the verbs in brackets. More than one tense may be possible.

   a This is the second time I (be) here.
   b Many years ago, I (see) the Taj Mahal. I've never forgotten it.
   c It was at least two years since we (speak) to each other.
   d (you / study) English for a long time?
   e Shakespeare (die) a very long time ago.
   f (you / write) any more poems since I last saw you?
   g It (rain) since Saturday morning and I'm fed up with it.
   h Tom and Louise (marry) for ten years.
   i I (have) a terrible headache for three days and then it went.
   j I (have) a headache since I woke up.

| 20 |

Fix it

Answers to Test it

Check your answers. Wrong answer?
Read the right Fix it note to find out why.

1
a	~~ate~~	've eaten	→	G
b	correct		→	B, E
c	~~since~~	for	→	B, E
d	~~I've been~~	I went	→	F
e	~~has died~~	died	→	D
f	~~since~~	for	→	B, E
g	~~trod~~	've trodden	→	G
h	correct		→	A, C
i	correct		→	E
j	correct		→	F

2
a	for	→ B		f	since	→ A
b	ago	→ F		g	for	→ B
c	since	→ A		h	since	→ A
d	since	→ A		i	for	→ B
e	ago	→ F		j	ago	→ F

Now go to page 23. Test yourself again.

Answers to Test it again

1
- a for two months
- b since 1999
- c for a couple of days
- d for two years
- e since last Saturday
- f since nine o'clock
- g for an hour
- h since last autumn
- i since September
- j since Christmas

2
- a 've been
- b saw
- c had spoken
- d Have you been studying/Have you studied/Did you study
- e died
- f Have you written
- g has been raining/has rained
- h have been married/were married
- i had
- j 've had

Fix it notes

A
Use *since* to say when something started. It can be a date, a time or an event.

B
Use *for* to say how long something went on or has been going on.

C
Use the past perfect in a main clause with *since* if the action is finished.

D
Use the past simple in a clause after *since* if the action is finished.

E
Use the present perfect or present perfect continuous with *for* if the action has a result in the present and you're talking about a length of time.

F
Use *ago* after a time reference with the past simple. Don't use the present perfect.

G
Use the present perfect with *This is the first/second/third time* …

For more information, see the Review page opposite. ▷

ⓘ Review

Since, for and *ago*

Since

- You use *since* to say when something started. This is a point in time,
  e.g. *Christmas, 1999, last Monday, I was ten*, etc.
  I haven't seen Johnny since Easter.
  Tom's been waiting for you since three o'clock.

- You use the present perfect in a main clause with *since* if the action has a result
  in the present and you're talking about when it started.
  She's been on a diet since last Wednesday.
  We've seen Emma twice since the weekend.

- You use the past perfect in a main clause with *since* if the action is finished.
  We'd met several times since that party.

- You use the past simple in a clause after *since* if the action is finished.
  We'd met several times since we were kids.

For

- You use *for* to say how long something went on or has been going on.
  David was at university for four years.
  Peter's been studying French for a month.

- You use the present perfect simple or continuous with *for* if the action has a
  result in the present and you're talking about a length of time.
  David has been at university for six months.
  (He's still at university now.)
  I've been reading this report for hours.
  (I'm still reading it.)

- You use the past simple with *for* if the action is finished.
  David was at university for four years.
  (He's left university now.)

Ago

- You use *ago* after a time period with the past simple.
  Luke and I met two weeks ago.   *I lived in Brussels ten years ago.*

This is the first time ...

- You use the present perfect with *This is the first/second/third time ...*
  This is the first time I've seen you.   *That's the second time you've lied to me!*

Past tenses

Test it ✓

❶ Choose the best option.

a   He's gone/He'd gone/He was going shopping. He'll be back soon.

b   We were late and the match started/had started/has started.

c   Teresa has never seen/never saw/was never seeing this film before.

d   They were having/had/have had a picnic when it started to rain.

e   Did you do/Have you done/Were you doing the washing-up yet?

f   He's wet because he swam/he's been swimming/he'd swum.

g   I crashed/I'd crashed/I've crashed your car last night. I'm really sorry.

h   Had you met/Have you met/Did you meet Jim Ward yesterday?

i   I'm/I was/I've been in Rome since June.

j   The dogs were barking and the kids had laughed/were laughing/have laughed
    as I walked into the room.

❷ Write the correct past tense form of the verbs in brackets.

a   Charlie (drive) when the accident happened.

b   What on earth (you / do)? You're covered in mud!

c   Marta (not / ride) a camel before and she was terrified.

d   (you / ever / see) the Taj Mahal? I hear it's incredibly beautiful.

e   How long (you / learn) English?

f   Our hamster (die) last week.

g   Shakespeare (write) poems as well as plays.

h   I (just / speak) to Jan. She told me the news.

i   The jury (not / agree) with the judge's decision.

j   I (read) a book when she called me.

20

GO to page 28 and check your answers.

Test it again ✔

1 **Find the correct sentence in each pair.**

a **A** I'm tired because I've trained for the marathon since six o'clock.
   B I'm tired because I've been training for the marathon since six o'clock.

b **A** I'm sorry. Jill's not here. She's been out.
   B I'm sorry. Jill's not here. She's gone out.

c **A** Sidney never met his father. He died just before he was born.
   B Sidney has never met his father. He died just before he was born.

d **A** Finally we found the shop but it had already closed.
   B Finally we found the shop but it already closed.

e **A** It was a hot summer's day and the birds sang.
   B It was a hot summer's day and the birds were singing.

f **A** Did you pay the gas bill last month?
   B Have you paid the gas bill last month?

g **A** I was playing the piano till I was twenty, then I gave it up.
   B I played the piano till I was twenty, then I gave it up.

h **A** Tara didn't believe a word Henry said.
   B Tara wasn't believing a word Henry said.

i **A** I was sure I'd met James before.
   B I was sure I met James before.

2 **Choose the best caption for the cartoon.**

I don't know who they belong to. They had followed me around all day!
I don't know who they belong to. They've been following me around all day!
I don't know who they belong to. They followed me around all day!

10

⚙ Fix it

Answers to Test it

Check your answers. Wrong answer?
Read the right Fix it note to find out why.

1
a He's gone → E
b had started → G
c has never seen → C
d were having → B
e Have you done → D
f he's been swimming → F
g crashed → A
h Did you meet → A
i I've been → E
j were laughing → B

2
a was driving → B
b have you been doing → F
c hadn't ridden → G
d Have you ever seen → C
e have you been learning → F
f died → A
g wrote → A
h 've just spoken → D
i didn't agree → A
j was reading → B

Now go to page 27. Test yourself again.

Answers to Test it again

1
a B   b B   c A   d A   e B
f A   g B   h A   i A   j A

2 I don't know who they belong to.
They've been following me around
all day!

⚙ Fix it notes

A
Use the past simple for completed
actions in the past.

B
Use the past continuous to talk about
past actions which weren't finished
at a past time or to describe what was
happening at a particular time in the past.

C
Use the present perfect simple (not the
past simple) to talk about general
experiences, especially when it isn't
important when something happened.

D
Use the present perfect simple (not the
past simple) to talk about recent past
events that have a result in the present.

E
Use the present perfect simple to talk
about an action that began in the past
but is still going on now.

F
Use the present perfect continuous
when the activity is important, or still
happening now.

G
Use the past perfect (not the past
simple) when one past action happened
before another past action.

For more information, see the
Review page opposite.

ⓘ Review

Past tenses

Past simple and continuous

*   You use the past simple for completed actions in the past, often with a time expression.
    We met in June 1998.   He didn't go to school yesterday.

*   You use the past continuous to talk about past actions which weren't finished at a past time or to describe what was happening at a particular time in the past. You use the past simple and past continuous together when one action interrupts another longer action in the past.
    What were they doing last night?   The sun was shining and a band was playing.
    As I was driving along, a cat ran into the road.

Present perfect simple and continuous

*   You use the present perfect to talk about general experiences. It isn't usually important when something happened.
    I've been to some wonderful places.   Have you ever used this software?

    Note: There's a difference in meaning between the participles *been* and *gone*.
    Yoichi has been to the States.   Yoichi has gone to the States.
    (He went to the States and now he's back.)   (He's in the States now.)

*   You use the present perfect (not the past simple) to talk about recent past events that have a result in the present.
    The plane has just landed at Heathrow.   Hasn't she finished that painting yet?

*   You use the present perfect to talk about an action that began in the past but is still going on now.
    We've lived in Singapore for a month. (We still live here.)

*   You use the present perfect continuous when you want to focus on the activity. The activity may still be going on now, or it may recently have finished.
    I've been writing emails all day.

Past perfect

*   You use the past perfect (not the past simple) when one past action happened before another past action.
    By the time we arrived, the plane had taken off.
    (First the plane took off, then we arrived.)

Note: You usually use the simple form (not the continuous form) with certain verbs, e.g. *believe, know, think, understand, want*, etc.
We haven't known each other long.

The future

Test it ✔

1 **Find and correct the mistake in each speech bubble.**

a
> If it'll rain on Saturday, we'll stay at home.

b
> Jane can't meet you tonight because she'll babysit for Sarah and Mike.

c
> I'm stopping eating all sugary things tomorrow.

d
> The plane takes off at 16.05 from Pisa and is landing at Heathrow at 18.05.

e
> Pete thinks his team is winning the match tomorrow.

f
> Kate's pregnant. She'll have a baby.

g
> My puppy is going to chew anything you give him. He destroys things all the time.

h
> I'll go shopping. Do you want to come?

2 **Write the correct form of the verbs in brackets.**

a I think Japan (win) the World Cup.
b When (you / be) back home? Do you have any idea?
c Look at those storm clouds. It (rain) most of the weekend.
d I (buy) my girlfriend a present. It's her birthday on Tuesday.
e That child never takes any exercise. He (be) very overweight.
f The bank has announced that interest rates (fall) next year.
g The class (start) at nine and finishes at eleven.
h I (visit) my Spanish friends soon. I've booked the ticket.
i If you don't stop that, I (call) the police.
j I (help) you. I'm good with computers.

18

GO to page 32 and check your answers.

Test it again ✔

1 **Choose the best option.**

a   I think I'm taking/I'll take Fred to the doctor. He's got a temperature.
b   Watch out! That ladder will/is going to fall on you.
c   Don't lend Beatrice your toys. She'll break/she's breaking them.
d   Patrick's going to/will read law at university.
e   We'll go/We're going out for a drink tonight. Do you fancy coming along?
f   If you don't study, you're failing/you'll fail your exams.
g   David's starting/going to start cycling to work. He wants to get fit.
h   This time next week, I'll be/I'm on the beach.
i   The ten o'clock news starts/will start in a minute.
j   Lucy and Jim will get married/are getting married on Saturday.

2 **Find the correct sentence in each pair.**

a   **A** You look tired. I'm washing up.
    B You look tired. I'll wash up.

b   **A** How old are you in 2035?
    B How old will you be in 2035?

c   **A** I can't come next weekend. I'm working.
    B I can't come next weekend. I'll work.

d   **A** Banks will win the election. I'm sure of it.
    B Banks is winning the election. I'm sure of it.

e   **A** Please go to Gate 19. The plane is going to take off at 14.20.
    B Please go to Gate 19. The plane takes off at 14.20.

3 **Choose the best caption for the cartoon.**

I'm going to be one of those when I grow up.
I'll be one of those when I grow up.
I'm one of those when I grow up.

16

Fix it

Answers to Test it

Check your answers. Wrong answer?
Read the right Fix it note to find out why.

1 **a** ~~'ll rain~~ rains → **H**
   b ~~'ll babysit~~ 's babysitting → **C**
   c ~~stopping~~ going to stop → **A**
   d ~~is landing~~ lands → **D**
   e ~~is winning~~
      will win/'s going to win → **F, B**
   f ~~'ll have~~
      's going to have → **B**
   g ~~is going to~~ will → **F**
   h ~~'ll go~~
      'm going (to go) → **A**

2 **a** will win → **F**
   b will you be → **G**
   c 's going to rain → **B**
   d 'm going to buy → **A**
   e 's going to be → **B**
   f will fall → **G**
   g starts → **D**
   h 'm going to visit → **A**
   i 'll call → **H**
   j 'll help → **E**

◀ Now go to page 31. Test yourself again.

Answers to Test it again

1 **a** I'll take
   b is going to
   c She'll break
   d 's going to
   e We're going out
   f you'll fail
   g going to start
   h I'll be lying
   i starts
   j are getting married

2 **a** B **b** B **c** A **d** A **e** B

3 I'm going to be one of those when
I grow up.

 Fix it notes

A
Use *going to* to talk about general plans
you've already made for the future.

B
Use *going to* to make a prediction
about the future based on something
you know or can see now.

C
Use the present continuous to talk
about fixed plans and arrangements
you've made for the future, especially
when you mention a time or place.

D
Use the present simple to talk about
timetabled or scheduled events.

E
Use *will* to make a decision at the
moment you speak.

F
Use *will* (*'ll*) and *won't* to say what you
think or guess will happen in the future.

G
Use *will* (*'ll*) and *won't* to talk about
future facts, or to ask questions about
the future.

H
Use *will* to talk about future possibilities
in first conditional sentences. Use the
present tense in the *if* clause and *will* or
won't in the other clause.

> For more information, see the
> Review page opposite. ▷

ℹ Review

The future

Present simple and continuous

- You use the present simple to talk about official fixed timetables and scheduled events, e.g. train timetables, TV programmes, cinema schedules, etc. You use the present continuous to talk about personal plans and arrangements you've made for the future. Often you mention the time or place.
  Spiderman starts at 17.10.   *When does the coach arrive in Bristol?*
  I'm meeting my brother at ten. (That's what we arranged.)

Going to and *will*

- You use *going to* to talk about general plans you've already made for the future. You also use *going to* to make logical predictions about the future based on things you know or can see now.
  We're going to watch the match.   *She's pregnant. She's going to have a baby.*

- You can also ask questions with *going to* when you think that the person you're talking to probably knows the answer.
  What are you going to say to Sheila? (I expect you've thought about it.)

Note: Sometimes it doesn't matter whether you use the present continuous or *going to*. The meaning is the same. If you're in doubt, use *going to*.
I'm going to travel by coach to London.   *I'm travelling by coach to London.*

- You use *will* (*'ll*) to make a decision at the moment you speak. Often you're offering to do something for someone.
  I'll come with you.   *I'll get you a cup of coffee.*   *Pete will help you.*

- You use *will* (*'ll*) and *won't* to say what you think or to make a guess about the future. You can also use *will* (*'ll*) and *won't* to talk about future facts.
  You won't be at school next week. You'll be on holiday.   *I'll be 27 soon.*
  Baker will score the first goal. (That's what I think.)
  The dog will eat the biscuits. (That's what I guess. He's done it before.)

- You can also use *will* to ask questions about the future when you aren't sure whether the person you're talking to knows the answer.
  Do you think Ben will marry Jill? (What's your opinion?)

Note: Sometimes it's possible to use either *going to* or *will* with only a very small difference in meaning. If you're in doubt, follow the rules above.

- You use *will* and *won't* in first conditional sentences.
  If I go to France, I'll go and see Vincent. (It's possible that I'll go to France.)

Second and third conditionals

Test it ✔

1 **Choose the best option.**

a If I didn't/don't have to work, I'd spend all my time travelling.

b We wouldn't have been/won't be late if you hadn't forgotten your tie.

c If you took/take more exercise, you'd feel better.

d I'd lend/'ll lend you some money if I had any.

e If I am/were you, I'd laugh about it.

f If you win/won the lottery, would you tell me?

g If I win/won the lottery, I'd share it with you.

h I wouldn't have been/wasn't angry if you hadn't told me about it.

i If the captain saw/had seen the iceberg, he wouldn't have hit it.

j I'd babysit for you if I don't/didn't have a meeting.

2 **Complete the sentences with the correct form of the verbs in brackets.**

a If Lindsay .... (stop) smoking, she'd feel better.

b I'd go round and apologize at once if I .... (be) you.

c If I hadn't gone to the party, I .... (not / meet) you.

d We wouldn't have met Jeff if Simon .... (not / invite) us to the party.

e If Billy weren't so good-looking, I .... (not / fancy) him.

f What .... you .... (say) if you'd been at the meeting?

g If she .... (work) harder, she'd get better marks.

h I .... (not / know) about that book if you hadn't recommended it.

i If Guy .... (take) more exercise, he'd be thinner.

j If the train hadn't been delayed, we .... (not / miss) the lecture.

20

GO to page 36 and check your answers.

Test it again ✔

1 **Match the two halves of each sentence.**

a	If you'd thought about it,	**1**	you'd call her straightaway.
b	Steve would be lonely	**2**	if we hadn't got the tickets.
c	If the guard hadn't fallen asleep,	**3**	if he'd been there?
d	If I were a bird,	**4**	you wouldn't have said it.
e	What would you do	**5**	if you were me?
f	They'd have been upset	**6**	I'd enter the marathon.
g	How would he have felt	**7**	if he didn't have his dog.
h	If I had more energy,	**8**	I'd emigrate every winter.
i	If you loved her,	**9**	the car wouldn't have been stolen.
j	I'd take an aspirin	**10**	if I were you.

2 **Rewrite these statements as conditional sentences.**

a Life isn't easy. I haven't got any money.

....

b Eat more fruit. That's my advice.

....

c Barbara revised. She passed the exam.

....

d We were late. You lost your keys.

....

e You never email me so I don't email you.

....

15

🔧 Fix it

Answers to Test it

Check your answers. Wrong answer?
Read the right Fix it note to find out why.

1
a	didn't	→	A, E
b	wouldn't have been	→	D, F
c	took	→	A, E
d	'd lend	→	A, E
e	were	→	C
f	won	→	B, E
g	won	→	B, E
h	wouldn't have been	→	D, F
i	had seen	→	D, F
j	didn't	→	A, E

2
a	stopped	→	E
b	were	→	C
c	wouldn't have met	→	F
d	hadn't invited	→	F
e	wouldn't fancy	→	E
f	would ... have said	→	F
g	worked	→	E
h	wouldn't have known	→	F
i	took	→	E
j	wouldn't have missed	→	F

Now go to page 35. Test yourself again.

Answers to Test it again

1
| a 4 | b 7 | c 9 | d 8 | e 5 |
| f 2 | g 3 | h 6 | i 1 | j 10 |

2 *Possible answers*
a Life would be easy if I had some
money.
b If I were you, I'd eat more fruit.
c If Barbara hadn't revised, she
wouldn't have passed the exam.
d We wouldn't have been late if
you hadn't lost your keys.
e If you emailed me, I'd email you.

🔧 Fix it notes

A
Use second conditional sentences when
you're thinking about present
situations.

B
Use second conditional sentences when
you're thinking about future situations.

C
Use second conditional sentences with
If I were you to give advice.

D
Use third conditional sentences to talk
about things that have already
happened in the past.

E
Use the past tense in the *if* clause of
second conditional sentences and
would/wouldn't in the other clause.

F
Use the past perfect in the *if* clause
of third conditional sentences and
would/wouldn't have in the other
clause.

For more information, see the
Review page opposite. ▷

 Review

Second and third conditionals

For information about zero and first conditional sentences, see *Test it, Fix it: English Verbs and Tenses Pre-intermediate* pages 53 and 61.

Second conditional

*   You can use second conditional sentences to talk about unreal situations in the present. You use the past tense in the *if* clause and *would/wouldn't* in the other clause.
    If I didn't have to work, I'd lie on the beach all day. (But I have to work, so I can't.)
    If we had lots of time, we'd travel. (But we haven't, so we don't.)

*   You can also use second conditional sentences to talk about unlikely events in the future.
    If I won the lottery, I'd share it with you.
    (But I probably won't win it, so I won't share it with you.)
    If I saw a ghost, I'd speak to it.
    (But I'm not very likely to see a ghost, so I won't speak to one.)

*   You can use second conditional sentences with *If I were you* to give advice.
    If I were you, I'd see a doctor.   *I wouldn't forget Jo's birthday if I were you.*

Third conditional

*   You use third conditional sentences to talk about things that have already happened in the past and their consequences. You use the past perfect in the *if* clause and *would/wouldn't have* in the other clause.
    If we hadn't smashed the car up, we wouldn't have got into trouble.
    (But we did smash the car up and we did get into trouble.)
    If I'd told you, you'd have been furious with me.
    (So I didn't tell you and you weren't furious.)

*   The *if* clause often comes first in conditional sentences. However, you can reverse the two clauses without changing the meaning.
    If James didn't have such a good sense of humour, I wouldn't like him as much. = I wouldn't like James as much if he didn't have such a good sense of humour.

*   When the *if* clause comes first, you put a comma between the two clauses. You don't need one if it comes second. Note, however, that native speakers often leave the comma out. You may see examples of this in newspapers and magazines, and on the internet.
    If it rained, I'd stay at home.   *I'd stay at home if it rained.*

Reported speech (1)

Test it ✔

① **Find the incorrect sentences.**

a   Sue told me she enjoys last night's party.
b   Carol asked what the time was.
c   Keith said he can hear me but there was a funny noise on the line.
d   Bill said I speak French. He's lived in Toulouse for five years.
e   They asked if we'd be at home.
f   The man asked me what was my name.
g   He said me he loved me.
h   I called Mick last Saturday. He said he'd seen Pete yesterday.
i   Tom asked where did I live.
j   The kids said they were happy.

② **Complete the reported speech.**

a   'I'm going to Hull tomorrow.' (said on Friday)
    Hilary said she was going to Hull .... (reported on Tuesday)
b   'Bordeaux is in south-west France.'
    Tony told me .... in south-west France.
c   'How old are you?'
    Mr Jones asked ....
d   'We can't find our cat!' (said on Saturday)
    The children said they .... cat. (reported on Sunday)
e   'Do you read poetry?'
    Julie asked me .... poetry.

15

GO to page 40 and check your answers.

Test it again ✔

1 **Rewrite the sentences as reported speech. Imagine you're reporting them a week later.**

a 'I'll be at the office tomorrow.'   He said ....

b 'Has Martin sent the letter?'   I asked .... the letter.

c 'Mars is called the Red Planet.'   She told us .... the Red Planet.

d 'Do you prefer red or white wine?'   He asked her .... red or white wine.

e 'Where's the hospital?'   They asked us ....

f 'The President has been shot!'   She said ....

g 'We went to John's house yesterday.'   He told me ....

h 'When did you get back?'   She asked me ....

i 'Do chickens have teeth?'   The child asked .... teeth.

j 'This mobile can't be working.'   He said ....

2 **Complete the sentences. Use one word in each space.**

a James .... me he was nervous.

b My son asked me .... I dreamt in colour.

c Ian asked me where the post office ....

d My dad said he .... call me at ten but he didn't.

e Natalie .... she felt unwell.

f The twins told us they couldn't find .... school uniforms.

g Colette asked if I'd seen Adam the day ....

h Help! I told you I .... swim!

i Ben said he .... marry me. The wedding's planned for June next year.

j Jill asked me .... old I was.

20

⚙ Fix it

Answers to Test it

Check your answers. Wrong answer?
Read the right Fix it note to find out why.

1   **a** ~~she enjoys~~ she'd enjoyed → **A**
    b correct   → **F**
    c ~~can~~   could   → **B**
    d ~~I speak~~
       he spoke/speaks   → **C, A**
    e correct   → **G**
    f ~~what was my name~~
       what my name was   → **F**
    g ~~He said me~~
       He told me/He said   → **E**
    h ~~yesterday~~ the day before → **D**
    i ~~where did I live~~
       where I lived   → **F**
    j correct   → **A**

2   **a** the following/next day.   → **D**
    b (that) Bordeaux was/is   → **A**
    c how old I was/am.   → **F**
    d couldn't find their   → **B, C**
    e if/whether I read   → **G**

> **Now go to page 39. Test yourself again.**

Answers to Test it again

1   **a** (that) he'd be at the office the
       following/next day.
    b if/whether Martin had sent
    c (that) Mars was/is called
    d if/whether she preferred/prefers
    e where the hospital was/is.
    f (that) the President had been shot.
    g (that) they'd been to John's house
       the day before/the previous day.
    h when I'd got back.
    i if/whether chickens had/have
    j (that) the mobile couldn't be
       working.

2   **a** told, **b** whether/if, **c** was/is,
    d would, **e** said, **f** their, **g** before,
    h couldn't/can't, **i** would, **j** how

⚙ Fix it notes

A
Usually go back a tense when you
report speech.

B
Change *can* to *could* and *will* to *would*
in reported speech.

C
Change the pronouns when you report
speech.

D
Change words like *today*, *tomorrow*,
etc. if the time period has changed.

E
Always put a personal direct object or
someone's name after *tell*. Never put a
personal direct object after *say*.

F
Use normal word order (subject + verb)
to report questions with a question
word. Don't use *do* and *don't, did* and
didn't.

G
Use *if* or *whether* to report *yes/no*
questions.

> For more information, see the
> Review page opposite. ▷

 Review

Reported speech

Reporting statements

- When you report speech, you usually need to go back a tense. See *Test It, Fix It: English Verbs and Tenses Pre-intermediate* page 81 for further details.
  'I'm hungry.'   *She said she was hungry.*
  'We've been to Rome.'   *They said they'd been to Rome.*
  Note that the past perfect doesn't change. It remains past perfect. Note also that you can use *that* in reported speech or you can leave it out.
  Zack told me (that) he'd fallen over.   *Belinda said (that) she was hungry.*

- If the situation is still true, it isn't always necessary to go back a tense. However, you'll always be right if you go back a tense so if you're in doubt, change the present to the past.
  'The earth is round.'   *The teacher said that the earth is/was round.*

- You change *can* to *could* and *will* to *would* in reported speech.
  'I can/can't see you!'   *He said he could/couldn't see me.*
  'I'll/I won't call you.'   *She said she'd/she wouldn't call me.*

- You usually need to change the pronouns when you report speech.
  'We can't find our toys.'   *They said they couldn't find their toys.*

- Words like *today, tomorrow, next Saturday, next year*, etc. also change if the time period has changed.
  'We're going to France today.' (said on Tuesday)
  They said they were going to France that day. (said on Saturday)

- Always put a personal direct object or someone's name after *tell*. Never put a personal direct object after *say*.
  Peter told me/Ann he was happy.   NOT   *Peter told he was happy.*
  Peter said he was happy.   NOT   *Peter said me he was happy.*

Reporting questions

- When you're reporting questions with a question word (*who, what, where, when, whose, how*), you use normal word order: subject + verb. Don't use *do* and *don't, did* and *didn't.*
  'Where are you?'   *She asked me where I was.*   NOT   *where was I.*
  'Where do you live?'   *She asked me where I lived.*   NOT   *where did I live.*

- When you're reporting *yes/no* questions, you use *if* or *whether*. It doesn't matter which you use. They mean the same thing.
  'Did Patrick go to Beijing?'   *He asked me if/whether Patrick had gone to Beijing.*

Reported speech (2)

Test it ✔

1 Choose the correct option, **A** or **B**.

a Alan suggested .... a film.
   A to see   **B** seeing

b He promised .... me.
   A emailing   **B** to email

c They ordered him .... them his passport.
   A to show   **B** showing

d I .... Tony to phone me when he arrived.
   A said   **B** told

e The man told us it .... later.
   A might have rained   **B** might rain

2 Choose the correct sentence in each pair.

a Let's go out for a meal.
   A I suggested him to go out for a meal.
   B I suggested going out for a meal.

b Don't shout.
   A Harry told me to not shout.
   B Harry told me not to shout.

c You'd better go.
   A Matthew said Ellen had better go.
   B Matthew said Ellen had better have gone.

d Sit down.
   A The teacher told the kids sit down.
   B The teacher told the kids to sit down.

e You should go to the dentist.
   A He thought she should go to the dentist.
   B He thought she should have gone to the dentist.

10

GO to page 44 and check your answers.

Test it again ✔

❶ Rewrite these sentences as reported speech.

a 'You should see a doctor.'

They told her ....

b 'Go and do some work.'

I advised him ....

c 'Sit down!'

The teacher ordered the boy ....

d 'We might come back later.'

They said ....

e 'Could you open the door?'

Leo asked me ....

f 'Why don't we go to the beach?'

Nick suggested ....

g 'I couldn't read the sign.'

She said ....

h 'We'll be back by ten.'

They promised ....

i 'Please, please lend me your bike.'

Dan begged Alan ....

j 'OK, I'll pick the kids up at six.'

Jules agreed ....

❷ Rewrite the reported speech as direct speech.

a He said I'd better go because it was late.

b She promised to give up smoking.

c He told me I ought to take the cat to the vet's.

d They said they could see us on Saturday.

e The officer said I mustn't drive so fast.

f Sid begged me not to tell anyone.

g The weatherman warned us it might snow.

h George and Isabelle suggested trying the new café.

i The traffic warden ordered me to move my car.

j I told her to wait for me.

20

Fix it

Answers to Test it

Check your answers. Wrong answer?
Read the right Fix it note to find out why.

1 a B → **B**   d B → **B**
    b B → **A**   e B → **C**
    c A → **A**

2 The correct sentences are:
    a B → **B**   d B → **A**
    b B → **A**   e A → **C**
    c A → **C**

Now go to page 43. Test yourself again.

Answers to Test it again

1 a They told her she should see a
    doctor.
  b I advised him to go and do some
    work.
  c The teacher ordered the boy to sit
    down.
  d They said they might come back
    later.
  e Leo asked me to open the door.
  f Nick suggested going to the beach.
  g She said she couldn't read the sign.
  h They promised to be back by ten.
  i Dan begged Alan to lend him his
    bike.
  j Jules agreed to pick the kids up
    at six.

2 a You'd better go because it's late.
  b I promise to give up/I'll give up
    smoking.
  c You ought to take the cat to the
    vet's.
  d We could see you on Saturday.
  e You mustn't drive so fast.
  f Please don't tell anyone.
  g It might snow.
  h Let's/Why don't we try the new
    café?
  i Move your car!
  j Wait for me.

Fix it notes

A

Use the infinitive or object + infinitive
to report orders and promises. In
negative statements, *not* goes between
the object and the infinitive.

B

Don't use the infinitive or object +
infinitive after the reporting verbs *say*
and *suggest*.

C

The verb after *would, could, should,
ought to, must, might* and *had better*
doesn't usually change its form after
past reporting verbs.

For more information, see the
Review page opposite.

ⓘ Review

Reported speech (2)

Orders, requests, promises, etc.

- You can use the infinitive or object + infinitive to report orders, requests, promises, offers, advice, agreements, etc.

'I'll write!'	Jill promised to write.
'We'll wash up for you.'	They offered to do the washing-up.
'Keep quiet!'	Mr Sykes ordered the children to keep quiet.
'You shouldn't call again.'	He advised me not to call again.

  In negative statements *not* goes between the object and the infinitive.
  She told me not to do it.   NOT   ~~She told me to not do it.~~

Say and *suggest*

- You don't use the infinitive or object + infinitive after the reporting verbs *say* and *suggest*. Use *told* or *suggest* + *-ing* form.

He told me to leave.	NOT	~~He said me to leave.~~
Mum told us not to go to the park.	NOT	~~Mum said us not to go to the park.~~
I suggested trying the new café.	NOT	~~I suggested to try the new café.~~
They suggested using their car.	NOT	~~They suggested us to use their car.~~

Would, could, should, etc.

- You don't usually change the form of the verbs after *would, could, should, ought to, must, might* and *had better* after past reporting verbs.

'I could buy some fruit.'	She said she could buy some fruit.
NOT	~~She said she could have bought some fruit.~~
'You'd better stay the night.'	He told me I'd better stay the night.
NOT	~~He told me I'd better have stayed the night.~~

The passive (1)

Test it ✔

1 **Which answer is best, A or B?**

a Do these computers come from Japan or Taiwan?
  A People make them in Taiwan.
  B They're made in Taiwan.

b So, what happened when the dog saw the bone?
  A It was eaten by the dog.
  B The dog ate it.

c How often is the restaurant kitchen cleaned?
  A People clean it every day.
  B It's cleaned every day.

d What happened to the burglar?
  A He was arrested a few minutes later.
  B The police arrested him a few minutes later.

e What do doctors do?
  A They help people who are sick.
  B People who are sick are helped by them.

2 **Find the incorrect sentences.**

a The money was stole from the bank.
b My house is being painted at the moment.
c I like it when people agree with me.
d The candidates are being interviewed.
e My friend Tom is having a nice house.
f You know, you are resembled by someone famous.
g Spanish spoken in Latin America.
h A lovely swim in the sea was had by us.
i These glasses are made in Denmark.
j Did your family agree with you?

15

GO to page 48 and check your answers.

Test it again ✔

① **Write passive sentences.**

  a Someone sells tickets at the box office.

    Tickets are sold at the box office.

  b People built the pyramids over 4,500 years ago.

    ....

  c Someone is mending my bike.

    ....

  d A printer printed the document in three seconds.

    ....

  e Someone's interviewing the President.

    ....

② **Rewrite the notices as active sentences. Start each sentence with *We*.**

  a   Secretary wanted

  b   Keys cut **while you wait**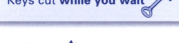

  c   Photos developed in one hour!

  d   *No* refunds given

  e   **CHEF** needed for busy restaurant

③ **Find and correct any sentences that are wrong.**

  a Made in China.
  b I'm not fitted by these trousers. They're too big.
  c The fox was knocked down by a car.
  d The tanks are filled and then the engine is started.
  e Stop arguing. I'm agreed with you!

15

Fix it

Answers to Test it

Check your answers. Wrong answer?
Read the right Fix it note to find out why.

1
a	B → **B**		d	A → **C**
b	B → **D**		e	A → **D**
c	B → **B**			

2
a	~~was stole~~	stolen	→	A
b	correct		→	B
c	correct		→	E
d	correct		→	B
e	~~is having~~	has	→	E
f	~~are resembled by~~			
	resemble		→	E
g	~~spoken~~	is spoken	→	A
h	~~A … was had by us.~~			
	We had … a		→	E
i	correct		→	B
j	correct		→	E

> **Now go to page 47. Test yourself again.**

Answers to Test it again

1
a Tickets are sold at the box office.
b The pyramids were built over 4,500 years ago.
c My bike is being mended.
d The document was printed in three seconds.
e The President is being interviewed.

2
a We want a secretary.
b We cut keys while you wait.
c We develop photos in one hour.
d We don't give refunds.
e We need a chef for a busy restaurant.

3
a correct
b ~~I'm not fitted by these trousers.~~
These trousers don't fit me.
c correct
d correct
e ~~I'm agreed with you!~~
I agree with you!

Fix it notes

A
Make the passive with the correct tense of the verb *be* + past participle.

B
Use the passive when you don't know who does the action, or you aren't interested in who does it, or it isn't important who does it.

C
Use the passive when it's obvious who does the action.

D
Always use the active form unless there's a very good reason to use the passive.

E
Don't use the passive with certain verbs, e.g. *agree with, have, resemble*.

> For more information, see the Review page opposite.

 **Review**

Active or passive?

Some people think the passive in English is difficult. It isn't really. You just need to understand why and when to use it instead of the active. There are four main reasons for using the passive, and these are explained below. It's also important to know when not to use the passive. There are two main reasons for you to remember.

- You make the passive with the correct tense of the verb *be* + past participle.
  Spanish is spoken in many Latin American countries. (present simple passive)
  My house is being painted. (present continuous passive)
  The robber was arrested. (past simple passive)

- The object of an active sentence becomes the subject of a passive sentence.
  People give money to charity. (object: money)
  Money is given to charity. (subject: money)

When to use the passive

1 When you don't know who does the action.
   My car was stolen last night. (I don't know who stole it.)

2 When you aren't interested in who does the action.
   I love this poem. It was written about a hundred years ago.
   (I'm interested in the poem, not the poet.)

3 When it isn't important who does the action.
   All our computers are checked before they leave the factory.
   (It isn't important who checks them.)

4 When it's obvious who does the action.
   The prisoner is being taken to the jail.
   (It's obvious that the police are taking him to jail.)

When not to use the passive

1 You don't use the passive when the active is more direct and easier to understand. If you're in doubt, ask yourself why you're using the passive instead of the active. If you can't think of a good reason, don't use it.
   I'm reading a great book.   NOT   ~~A great book is being read by me.~~

2 Intransitive verbs can't be passive because they don't take an object, e.g. *arrive, die, sit, sleep*. Also, you don't use the passive with these verbs: *agree with, belong, fit, have, resemble* and *suit*.
   Unfortunately, he died.   NOT   ~~Unfortunately, he was died.~~
   The dog has a basket.   NOT   ~~A basket is had by the dog.~~

The passive (2)

Test it ✓

❶ Choose the best sentence in each pair.

a A new job has been offered to Luke.
b Luke's been offered a new job.

c No directions were given to us.
d We weren't given any directions.

e This is a lovely piece of music. Someone composed it in 1790.
f This is a lovely piece of music. It was composed in 1790.

g Polly is a poet. A new book of poems has just been written by her.
h Polly is a poet. She's just written a new book of poems.

i A thief committed a theft in New Street last night.
j A theft was committed in New Street last night.

k 100% cotton. Made in Egypt.
l 100% cotton. People in Egypt made it.

m A full refund was given to me.
n I was given a full refund.

o No one wants to be forgotten.
p People don't want people to forget them.

q Basil Morgan taught me history.
r History was taught to me by Basil Morgan.

s The pupils were punished for cheating.
t The teacher punished the pupils for cheating.

❷ Write the correct passive form of the verbs in brackets.

a You (give) instructions when you arrive.
b I suddenly realized I (watch).
c When we got back to the car, we found that it (vandalize).
d Carmen (interview) for the job right now.
e The van Dyck painting (sell) at auction next year.
f I (teach) French by Malcolm Smith at university.
g I'm sorry it's so noisy. Our new kitchen (fit).
h The school (open) by the Prince next Tuesday.
i Spanish (speak) in Latin America.
j Ten thousand of these cars (make) in France every year.

20

GO to page 52 and check your answers.

Test it again ✔

1 **Write passive sentences. Include a *by* phrase only if you think it's necessary.**

a When we arrived a waiter was serving dinner.

....

b The mother gave birth to George on 4 October.

....

c Dufy painted this picture.

....

d Auctioneers will sell the painting at auction.

....

e Someone's offered me a better job.

....

f They're taking the goods to market.

....

g Someone owes me a lot of money.

....

h The police have arrested the mugger.

....

i By the time I got back, someone had ordered the coffee.

....

j I'm sure my uncle invented this machine.

....

2 **Rewrite these sentences. Keep the same meaning.**

a The prize was awarded to me!   I ....

b The police stopped Phil for speeding.   Phil ....

c Somebody built this monument in 1716.   This ....

d Documents were given to me to sign.   I ....

e Someone warned him not to do it.   He ....

15

Fix it

Answers to Test it

Check your answers. Wrong answer?
Read the right Fix it note to find out why.

1 The best sentences are:

b → E		k → B
d → E		n → E
f → B		o → B
h → D		q → D
j → C		s → C

2
a will be given	→	A
b was being watched	→	A
c had been vandalized	→	A
d 's being interviewed	→	A
e will/is going to be sold	→	A
f was taught	→	A
g is being fitted	→	A
h will/is going to be opened	→	A
i is spoken	→	A
j are made	→	A

Now go to page 51. Test yourself again.

Answers to Test it again

1
a Dinner was being served when we arrived.
b George was born on 4 October.
c This picture was painted by Dufy.
d The painting will be sold at auction.
e I've been offered a better job.
f The goods are being taken to market.
g I'm owed a lot of money.
h The mugger has been arrested.
i By the time I got back, the coffee had been ordered.
j I'm sure this machine was invented by my uncle.

2
a I was awarded the prize!
b Phil was stopped for speeding.
c This monument was built in 1716.
d I was given documents to sign.
e He was warned not to do it.

Fix it notes

A
Make the passive with the correct tense of the verb *be* + past participle.

B
Use the passive when you don't know who does the action, or you aren't interested in who does it, or it isn't important who does it.

C
Use the passive when it's obvious who does the action.

D
Always use the active form unless there's a very good reason to use the passive.

E
If a verb has two objects, usually use the person as the subject in the passive.

For more information, see the Review page opposite.

 Review

The passive (2)

- You make the passive with the correct tense of the verb *be* + past participle.

	Active	Passive
Present	People owe me money.	I am owed some money.
Past simple	Matisse painted this.	This was painted by Matisse.
Past continuous	They were taking him away.	He was being taken away.
Present perfect	I've sold the car.	The car has been sold.
Past perfect	He'd ordered coffee.	Coffee had been ordered.
Future	We'll read the report.	The report will be read.

- You use the passive when you don't know who does the action, or you aren't interested in who does it, or it isn't important who does it.
  The poem was written in 1675.   *The carpets were cleaned.*
  (I don't know who wrote it.)   (It isn't important who cleaned them.)

- You use the passive when it's obvious who does the action.
  The theft was committed at 02.35.   *He's been arrested.*
  (It's obvious a thief committed the theft.)   (It's obvious the police arrested him.)

- Always use the active form unless there's a very good reason to use the passive.
  I've been offered a fantastic job.   NOT   ~~A fantastic job has been offered to me.~~

- You use *by* + agent (person or thing) if you want to say who does the action. Sometimes it's important to say who did it.
  This statue was created by Henry Moore.
  The 'Difference Engine' was invented by Charles Babbage.

- If a verb has two objects, you usually use the person as the subject in the passive.

Active	*No one gave me any directions.*
Passive	*I wasn't given any directions.* (more common)
	No directions were given to me.
Active	*Basil taught me history.*
Passive	*I was taught history by Basil.* (more common)
	History was taught to me by Basil.

Have/Get something done

Test it ✔

❶ Match the statements.

a	I got the car serviced.	**1**	She paid someone to paint it.
b	She had her hair cut.	**2**	He's a photographer.
c	He'll develop the film.	**3**	We're the victims of a burglary.
d	Pam painted her house.	**4**	She went to the hairdresser's.
e	I serviced the car.	**5**	I went to a garage.
f	Our house was burgled.	**6**	We're burglars.
g	He'll have the film developed.	**7**	She cut it herself.
h	We burgled the house.	**8**	She likes painting.
i	She cut her hair.	**9**	He'll take it to the camera shop.
j	Pam had her house painted.	**10**	I'm a mechanic.

❷ Find the best sentence in each pair.

a Sarah went to the hairdresser's and her hair was cut.
b Sarah went to the hairdresser's and had her hair cut.

c My house was burgled.
d I had the house burgled.

e It's time we serviced our car.
f It's time we had our car serviced.

g Jack painted my kitchen.
h My kitchen was painted by a painter.

i Our window was smashed last night.
j We had our window smashed last night.

15

GO to page 56 and check your answers.

Test it again ✓

① Write the correct form of *have* + the object in brackets + a suitable participle from the list.

coloured	*restrung*	*trimmed*	*painted*	*put up*
valued	*mended*	*taken*	*drawn up*	*broken into*

a I wonder what this bracelet is worth. I think I'll (it).
b Shall we (the baby's room) blue or pink?
c You really must (your guitar). It sounds terrible!
d I (the contract) last week.
e Next spring we (the roof).
f Your hair's looking rather grey. When did you last (it)?
g Gregory never (his beard). It drives me crazy.
h I'd like to (some shelves). There isn't enough room for my books.
i You ever (your picture) by a professional photographer?
j That's the second time we (garden shed). Next time, I'll call the police.

② Choose the best option, A or B.

a Keith .... playing football. He was running too fast.
　　A broke his leg **B** 's leg was broken
b Janine .... on her parents' land.
　　A built a small house **B** had a small house built
c I'm sorry but ....
　　A I crashed the car **B** I had the car crashed
d Lucy went to the beautician's and ....
　　A her nails were painted **B** had her nails painted
e Tim .... once a year.
　　A 's house is decorated **B** has his house decorated

15

🔧 Fix it

Answers to Test it

Check your answers. Wrong answer?
Read the right Fix it note to find out why.

1   a 5 → **A**   f 3 → **B**
      b 4 → **A**   g 9 → **A**
      c 2 → **C**   h 6 → **C**
      d 8 → **C**   i 7 → **C**
      e 10 → **C**   j 1 → **A**

2 The best sentences are:
      b → **A**   g → **C**
      c → **B**   i → **B**
      f → **A**

◄ Now go to page 55. Test yourself again.

Answers to Test it again

1 a have it valued
     b have the baby's room painted
     c have your guitar restrung
     d had the contract drawn up
     e have the roof mended
     f have it coloured
     g has his beard trimmed
     h have some shelves put up
     i had your picture taken
     j had our garden shed broken into

2 a A   b B   c A   d B   e B

🔧 Fix it notes

A

Use *have* (or *get*) + object + past
participle to say that you arrange for
someone to do something for you.

B

Use the passive (object + *be* + past
participle) when something happens
that you didn't arrange.

C

Use the active (subject + verb + object)
when the subject does the action.

> For more information, see the
> Review page opposite. ▷

 **Review**

Have/Get something done

Unlike some other languages, in English you can't say that you do, did or will do something if you mean that someone else does the action. So, for example, you can't say 'I'm going to service the car' if you mean that you're going to take it to a garage and a mechanic is going to service it for you. Instead, you can use the structure *have/get something done*: 'I'm going to have the car serviced.'

- You use *have* (or *get*) + object + past participle to say that you arrange for someone to do something for you. Often it's a service that you pay for.
  I'm having my hair cut next week.   *Let's get the dog shampooed.*

  Note that *get* is more informal than *have* but the meaning is the same.
  I'm going to get my computer fixed. = I'm going to have my computer fixed.

- You use the passive (object + correct form of *be* + past participle) when something happens that you didn't arrange and didn't want.
  Our house was broken into last night.
  (I didn't arrange for this to happen.)
  My wallet was stolen in the shopping centre.

- You can also use *have* + object + past participle to talk about experiences. Often these experiences are unpleasant.
  Peter had his motorbike stolen last summer.
  (He didn't arrange for this to happen. It was something that happened to him.)
  We've had our car vandalized five times this year.

- You use the active (subject + verb + object) when the subject does the action.
  I cut my hair last night. It looks a mess!   *John's repaired my computer.*
  (I did it myself.)   (He's a computer engineer.)

- You can use *have/get* + object + past participle in all tenses.
  I'm having my hair cut at the moment.
  I have my car serviced twice a year.
  I was having the house valued when he arrived.
  I had the window mended.
  I've had my house broken into twice.
  I've been having the kitchen painted.
  I'd had my portrait painted once before.
  I'd been having my films processed there for years.
  I'm going to have the dog shampooed.
  I'll have this jacket dry-cleaned, please.

Relative clauses

Test it ✔

1 **Find and correct the mistake in each sentence.**

a   The man which I met is a lawyer.

b   Ian, mother lives next door to me, is emigrating to South Africa.

c   The rabbit hutch what I built is falling to pieces.

d   The book, that you lent me is great.

e   Is that the girl you told me about her?

f   The farm, who I lived in for nearly twenty years, has been sold.

g   A corkscrew is a thing who you open bottles with.

h   He's the guy which sold me my house.

i   Henry, which is a friend of my brother's, is coming to the party.

j   This is the translator who I met her in London.

2 **Write *who, that, which, where* or *whose* where necessary. Sometimes more than one answer is possible.**

a   Isn't that the boy .... gave you the flowers?

b   This village, ... John was brought up, is now a tourist attraction.

c   The mobile phone, ... you promised to deliver yesterday, still hasn't arrived.

d   I really wanted the car .... you bought.

e   What's the name of that girl .... father is a vet?

15

GO to page 60 and check your answers.

Test it again ✔

1 **Choose the best option.**

The man ᵃ who/which everyone was expecting finally arrived. He was wearing a dark suit ᵇ who/that made him look twice the size he really was. He looked odd. Everybody turned and stared at him. His moustache,ᶜ where/which was red and curly, moved slightly every time he spoke. A young woman, ᵈ which/whose face went white when she saw the man, suddenly fainted in a corner of the room. It was then that I began to understand! She was the woman ᵉ which/that he'd come to see. She was the Lady of Castle Doom.

2 **Write each pair of sentences as one sentence. Use defining and non-defining relative clauses.**

a That's the man. His car was vandalized.

....

b The laboratory is usually locked. It's a very big laboratory.

....

c 'The Liar' is a good book. Stephen Fry wrote it.

....

d He's the man. Kate told you about him.

....

e Thomas lives in Los Angeles. He is my cousin.

....

	10

Fix it

Answers to Test it

Check your answers. Wrong answer?
Read the right Fix it note to find out why.

1 **a** ~~which~~
   who/no pronoun   → **A, B**
   b ~~Ian, mother~~
   Ian, whose mother   → **C, B**
   c ~~what~~
   that/which/no pronoun   → **A, B**
   d ~~The book, that~~
   The book (that)   → **E, B**
   e ~~you told me about her?~~
   you told me about?   → **D**
   f ~~who~~   which   → **C**
   g ~~who~~
   that/which/no pronoun   → **A, B**
   h ~~which~~   who/that   → **A**
   i ~~which~~   who   → **C**
   j ~~I met her in London.~~
   I met in London.   → **D**

2 **a** who/that   → **A**
   b where   → **C**
   c which   → **C**
   d that/which/no pronoun   → **A, B**
   e whose   → **A**

◀ Now go to page 59. Test yourself again.

Answers to Test it again

1 **a** who   **d** whose
   b that   **e** that
   c which

2 **a** That's the man whose car was
      vandalized.
   b The laboratory, which is very big,
      is usually locked.
   c 'The Liar', which Stephen Fry
      wrote, is a good book.
   d He's the man (that/who) Kate told
      you about.
   e Thomas, who's my cousin, lives
      in Los Angeles.

Fix it notes

A
This sentence includes a defining
relative clause. Begin these clauses
with *who/that* for people; *that/which* for
objects; *where* for places; *whose* for
possession.

B
You can leave out *who, that, which,* etc.
in a defining relative clause that is the
object of the sentence. You can't leave
it out in a defining relative clause that is
the subject of the sentence. You can
never leave it out of a non-defining
relative clause.

C
This sentence includes a non-defining
relative clause. Begin these clauses with
who for people; *which* for objects;
where for places; *whose* for possession.

D
Don't use more than one subject or
object pronoun (*he, her,* etc.) in a
relative clause.

E
Use commas before and after non-
defining relative clauses. Don't use
them before and after defining relative
clauses.

For more information, see the
Review page opposite. ▷

 Review

Relative clauses

Defining relative clauses

- You use defining relative clauses to add essential information to a sentence. The clause goes immediately after the noun it describes.
  This is the man.   This is the man who sold me the car.
  *   (The clause answers the question 'which man?')*

- You use relative pronouns (*who, which, that*, etc.) to introduce defining relative clauses. Use *who* or *that* for people; *that* or *which* for objects; *where* to talk about a place; *whose* to talk about possession.
  He's the man who/that owns the shop.   Here's the book that/which you lent me.
  This is the place where I was born.   He's the man whose dog bit me.

- You can leave out *who, that, which*, etc. in a defining relative clause when the clause is the object of the sentence.
  She's the girl (that) I told you about.   Here's the book (that) you lent me.
  You can't leave it out in a defining relative clause when the clause is the subject of the sentence.
  This is the man who got the job.   Rome is the city where I was born.
  You can never leave it out of a non-defining relative clause.
  The fans, who were waiting anxiously, finally saw the rock star.
  NOT   *The fans, were waiting anxiously, finally saw the rock star.*

- You don't use more than one subject or object pronoun in a relative clause. The relative pronoun (*who, which*, etc.) replaces the subject or object pronouns (*he, her*, etc.). One pronoun is enough.
  Jack's the boy who won the prize.   NOT   *Jack's the boy who he won the prize.*

Non-defining relative clauses

- You use non-defining relative clauses to add non-essential information to a sentence. The clause goes immediately after the noun it describes. If you removed the relative clause, the sentence would still make sense on its own.
  David, who is a professor at the University of Barcelona, is a friend of mine.
  Note that non-defining relative clauses are much more common in writing than they are in speech.

- You use relative pronouns (*who, which, where*, etc.) to introduce non-defining relative clauses. Use *who* for people; *which* for objects; *where* to talk about a place; *whose* to talk about possession.
  Paddy, who's my brother, trained as a lawyer.
  Harry, whose toys are lying all over the floor, is my puppy.
  Remember to use commas before and after non-defining relative clauses.

Modal verbs

Test it ✔

1 **Find the incorrect sentences.**

a   I think you should work harder.
b   Do you can speak Japanese?
c   Mary thinks it may rain later.
d   The twins must tidy their bedroom.
e   Sally musts go to the dentist soon.
f   I'm sorry but we must to go now.
g   That can't be the postman. It's much too early.
h   The dog didn't should steal food from the fridge.
i   We maying go to France in September.
j   Could you lend me your dictionary?

2 **Use a suitable modal to complete the sentences. Use some modals more than once. Sometimes there is more than one correct answer.**

can   can't   could   must   mustn't   shouldn't   may   might

a   I want the salt, please.   .... you pass me the salt, please?

b   It's a bad idea for you to go.   You .... go.

c   It's possible it'll rain tomorrow.   It .... rain tomorrow.

d   Do you have the ability to swim?   .... you swim?

e   Do not park here.   You .... park here.

f   Is it OK if I use your phone?   .... I use your phone?

g   That isn't a bird. It's impossible!   That .... be a bird!

h   It's important that you stop smoking.   You .... stop smoking.

i   It's possible I'll ask you to help me.   I .... ask you to help me.

j   Fred is unable to sing.   Fred .... sing.

20

GO to page 64 and check your answers.

Test it again ✔

❶ Choose the best option.

a Jeff may not/can't/might not ride a bicycle. He never learnt to do it.

b I'm sure you can't/couldn't/must be tired. You were awake all night.

c It might/can/must be a nice weekend. If it is, we'll go to the beach.

d May/Should/Could you close the window? I'm cold.

e Mobile phones can/must/might be switched off during the flight.

f You really should/could/might stop smoking.

g That can/should/can't be a spider. It's only got six legs.

h Tom isn't here. He can/may/shouldn't be at home.

i You shouldn't/couldn't/mustn't forget your passport this time!

j Drivers can/may/should go more slowly. There are too many accidents.

❷ Write new sentences with similar meanings, using modals. More than one answer may be possible.

a I want a glass of water.

....

b Lock the door, please.

....

c Do you want me to help you?

....

d No smoking in the library.

....

e It's possible that you're right.

....

❸ Find and correct five mistakes in the dialogue.

Jo: Bill musts be here soon. He left hours ago!

Nick: I think you should call him on the mobile. He must to have it with him.

Jo: I can't. My battery is flat. Must I borrow yours?

Nick: Yes, sure. Here you are.

Jo: No answer. Now what do I should do?

Nick: You should stop worrying. I'm sure he won't be long. He mays arrive any moment.

20

🔧 Fix it

Answers to Test it

Check your answers. Wrong answer?
Read the right Fix it note to find out why.

1
  a correct   → **F**
  b ~~Do you can~~   Can you   → **D**
  c correct   → **G**
  d correct   → **I**
  e ~~musts~~   must   → **A**
  f ~~must to go~~   must go   → **B**
  g correct   → **H**
  h ~~didn't should~~ shouldn't   → **D**
  i ~~maying~~   may   → **C**
  j correct   → **E**

2
  a Can/Could   → **E**
  b shouldn't   → **F**
  c may/might   → **G**
  d Can   → **E**
  e mustn't   → **I**
  f Can/Could/May   → **E**
  g can't   → **H**
  h must   → **I**
  i may/might/could   → **G**
  j can't   → **E**

▶ Now go to page 63. Test yourself again.

Answers to Test it again

1
  a can't   **f** should
  b must   **g** can't
  c might   **h** may
  d Could   **i** mustn't
  e must   **j** should

2
  a Can/Could/May I have a glass of water?
  b Can/Could you lock the door?
  c Can I help you?
  d You mustn't smoke in the library.
  e You may/might/could be right.

3
  ~~musts~~   must
  ~~must to have~~   must have
  ~~Must I?~~   Can/Could/May I?
  ~~do I should do~~   should I do
  ~~mays~~   may

🔧 Fix it notes

A
Never put *s* on the third person singular form of modal verbs.

B
Use the base form of the verb (not the *to* infinitive) after modal verbs.

C
Modal verbs haven't got infinitives or participles.

D
Make modal questions and negative sentences without *do*.

E
Use *can/can't* to talk about ability. Use *can, could* or *may* to ask for or give permission. Use *can/could you* to make a request.

F
Use *should/shouldn't* to ask for or give someone advice.

G
Use *may, might* and *could* to talk about possibilities.

H
Use *must* and *can't* to make logical deductions.

I
Use *must* and *mustn't* to talk about obligations.

For more information, see the Review page opposite. ▷

 Review

Modal verbs

- You never put *s* on the third person singular form of modal verbs.
  He can do it!   NOT   *He cans do it!*
  It might rain.   NOT   *It mights rain.*

- You use the base form of the verb, not the *to* infinitive, after modal verbs.
  I must go to the bank.   NOT   *I must to go to the bank.*
  Jo can't come tonight.   NOT   *Jo can't to come tonight.*

  Note that modal verbs haven't got infinitives or participles. You can't say 'to should' or 'maying' or 'musted'.

- You make modal questions and negative sentences without *do*.
  Can I help you?   NOT   *Do can I help you?*
  He shouldn't say that.   NOT   *He don't should say that.*

- You use *can/can't* to talk about ability.
  I can swim. He can't read.

- You use *can, could* or *may* to ask for or give permission. Note that *may* is more formal and less common than *can* or *could*. You also use *can* to ask for things.
  Can I stay up late tonight?   *Could we go out?*   *May I borrow your car?*
  Can I have a drink?

- You use *can/could you* to make a request.
  Can you shut the door?   *Could you pass me the salt?*

- You use *should/shouldn't* to ask for or give someone advice.
  What should I say to Mum?   *You should apologize.*   *You shouldn't do that.*

- You use *may, might* and *could* to talk about possibilities.
  It may rain during the night.   *Jack might be at home by now.*
  The keys could be in the car.

- You use *must* and *can't* to make logical deductions. Usually the deduction is based on something you know now.
  You must be hungry. I know you haven't eaten anything.
  That can't be an insect. It's got too many legs.

- You use *must* and *mustn't* to talk about obligations.
  Passengers must switch off their mobile phones.   *You mustn't park here.*

Modals in the past

Test it ✓

❶ Choose the best option.

a I tried and tried but I can't/couldn't open the jar.

b How nice of you to write and thank me. You really had to/needn't have.

c When we were at school we must/had to wear school uniform. We all hated it.

d I heard a noise. I think it must have/should have been the cat jumping through the window.

e You could have/would have laughed if you'd seen his face!

f I'm afraid I can't have/wasn't able to get in touch with George.

g You might have/can't have seen Tim. He left for the States last week.

h I think you should have/had to apologized to Samantha.

i I needn't/didn't have to work last Sunday. I had a day off.

j That letter must/might have arrived by now. I sent it yesterday.

❷ Find the incorrect sentences.

a You should have watched the film last night. It was great.

b I hadn't to go to work last week so I went to stay with friends.

c Pete must gone out. The door's locked.

d I would have got full marks if I'd studied a bit harder.

e We needn't to hurry – we had plenty of time.

f Jim can't swim till he was twelve.

g The phone was ringing when I came in. It might be Lisse.

h Did you must get up early when you worked on the farm?

i We shouldn't have stayed out so late. I'm tired now.

j Do you think that man we saw can have been the burglar?

20

GO to page 68 and check your answers.

Test it again ✓

❶ Complete the sentences. Use a modal from the list and the correct form of the verb in brackets.

might have   could have (x 2)   should have   had to
didn't have to   would have   needn't have

a What .... you .... (do) if you'd been me?

b I'm not sure but I think it .... (be) the postman who knocked just then.

c No one .... (predict) last night's thunderstorm. It was a total surprise.

d Do you think I .... (call) Nick?

e None of us .... (get up) early so we slept till eight.

f Phil .... (send) me these flowers but I'm glad he did!

g I think Tom .... (be) here. I think I saw his car.

h We .... (clean) the flat because the kids had already done it.

❷ True or false?

a Jo shouldn't have been so silly.
Jo wasn't silly.   True ☐   False ☐

b That must have been an eagle.
I'm sure it was an eagle.   True ☐   False ☐

c You couldn't have been there.
I'm sure you weren't there.   True ☐   False ☐

d I didn't have to go to school yesterday.
I probably went to school.   True ☐   False ☐

12

🔧 Fix it

Answers to Test it

Check your answers. Wrong answer?
Read the right Fix it note to find out why.

1
a couldn't	→	**G**
b needn't have	→	**D**
c had to	→	**C**
d must have	→	**A**
e would have	→	**H**
f wasn't able to	→	**G**
g can't have	→	**B**
h should have	→	**E**
i didn't have to	→	**C**
j might have	→	**F**

2
a correct	→	**E**
b ~~hadn't to~~ didn't have to	→	**C**
c ~~must gone~~		
must have gone	→	**A**
d correct	→	**H**
e ~~needn't to hurry~~		
needn't have hurried	→	**D**
f ~~can't~~ couldn't	→	**G**
g ~~might be~~		
might/could have been	→	**F**
h ~~Did you must~~		
Did you have to	→	**C**
i correct	→	**E**
j ~~can have been~~		
could have been	→	**F**

Now go to page 67. Test yourself again.

Answers to Test it again

1
a would you have done
b might have been/could have been
c could have predicted
d should have called
e had to get up
f needn't have sent
g might have been/could have been
h didn't have to clean

2
a False	**c** True
b True	**d** False

🔧 Fix it notes

A
Use *must have* + past participle to say that you believe that something was true in the past.

B
Use *can't/couldn't have* + past participle to say that you believe that something was impossible in the past.

C
Use *didn't have to/had to* to talk about things that weren't or were necessary in the past.

D
Use *needn't have* + past participle to say that something wasn't necessary in the past but that it happened anyway.

E
Use *should/shouldn't have* + past participle to say that something was the right or wrong thing to do in the past.

F
Use *might/could have* + past participle to say that something was a possibility.

G
Use *couldn't/could* and *wasn't able to/was able to* to talk about ability in the past.

H
Use *would/wouldn't have* + past participle in third conditional sentences.

For more information, see the Review page opposite. ⟶

 Review

Modals in the past

- You use *must have* + past participle to say that you believe that something was true in the past. You usually believe it was true because of something you know.
  It must have taken you ages to write that report. (I know it was a very long report.)
  It must have rained last night. (The ground is wet.)

- You use *can't/couldn't have* + past participle to say that you believe that something was impossible in the past. You usually believe it was impossible because of something you know.
  He can't have come home very late. (I was still awake when he came back.)
  He couldn't have committed the murder. (He was somewhere else at the time.)

- You use *had to* and *didn't have to* to talk about things that were or weren't necessary in the past.
  I had to leave at ten. (I had another meeting to get to.)
  I didn't have to wear a uniform at school. (The school rules didn't require it.)

- You use *needn't have* + past participle to say that something wasn't necessary in the past but that it happened anyway.
  You needn't have sent me the roses. (It wasn't necessary but I'm very grateful.)

- You *use should/shouldn't have* + past participle to say that something was the right or wrong thing to do in the past.
  You should have gone home. (It was the right thing to do but you didn't go.)
  He shouldn't have said that. (It was a bad thing to do but he did it.)

- You use *might/could have* + past participle to say that something was a possibility in the past.
  I think that might have been the postman. (I'm not sure but it's possible.)
  Jane could have sent me the chocolates. (It's possible it was Jane who sent them.)

- You use *could/couldn't* and *was/wasn't able to* to talk about ability in the past.
  I could/was able to read when I was four.
  He couldn't/wasn't able to swim till he was ten.

- You use *would/wouldn't have* + past participle in third conditional sentences.
  Tim would have helped you if he'd been here.
  (But he wasn't here so he didn't.)
  I wouldn't have gone out if I'd known it was raining.
  (But I did go out.)

Verb patterns

Test it ✔

1 **Complete the sentences. Use the correct form of the verbs in brackets.**

a You won't believe this! Jimmy wants me .... (go) out with him!

b Carla says she'd prefer .... (stay) in than go out tonight.

c Mike loves .... (chat) to new people.

d Are you interested in .... (play) tennis with me sometime?

e Sally denied .... (eat) the sweets even though it was obvious she had.

f Will you let us .... (watch) TV if we do our homework?

g My grandfather taught us .... (fish) with rods and nets.

h I regret .... (say) that I completely forgot your birthday. I won't next year.

i I'm sorry but I don't remember .... (meet) you before.

j What do you hope .... (be) when you grow up?

2 **Find and correct one mistake in each sentence.**

a I suggested to have a picnic at the weekend.

b She made me to do all the washing-up and make the beds!

c Tony always persuades me relaxing.

d I can't drink coffee without to put three spoonfuls of sugar in it.

e The lecturer let me to hand in my essay late.

f We stopped having lunch because we were hungry.

g So, what do you advise me doing?

h Jill will never forget to lose her son in the shopping centre.

i Please don't let me forgetting to post this letter.

j We all dislike to work here. The pay is terrible.

20

GO to page 72 and check your answers.

Test it again ✅

❶ Solve the clues to complete the crossword. Use the correct form of the verbs below.

tie   regret   laugh   like   revise   want   talk   enjoy
give   hope   see   prefer   remind   be   take

Across

3 Who wants to … a millionaire?
4 I'd … to pay in cash.
6 Stop … for a second, please!
9 We're looking forward to … you soon.
10 Would you … to go for a walk?
14 He suggested … the bus.
15 Please … me to pay the gas bill.

Down

1 I … to say that you're wrong this time.
2 I … to see you again one day.
5 She stopped to … her shoelaces.
7 Don't make me …!
8 Do you regret not … for the exam?
11 Do the kids … playing tennis?
12 Does Tom … to marry Gisella?
13 Jack persuaded his boss to … him a pay rise.

20

Answers to Test it

Check your answers. Wrong answer?
Read the right Fix it note to find out why.

1
a	to go	→ F	f	watch	→ G
b	to stay	→ C	g	to fish	→ F
c	chatting	→ B	h	to say	→ D
d	playing	→ A	i	meeting	→ E
e	eating	→ B	j	to be	→ C

2
a	~~to have~~	having	→ B
b	~~to do~~	do	→ G
c	~~relaxing~~	to relax	→ F
d	~~to put~~	putting	→ A
e	~~to hand in~~	hand in	→ G
f	~~having~~	to have	→ D
g	~~doing~~	to do	→ F
h	~~to lose~~	losing	→ E
i	~~forgetting~~	forget	→ G
j	~~to work~~	working	→ B

◄ Now go to page 71. Test yourself again.

Answers to Test it again

1

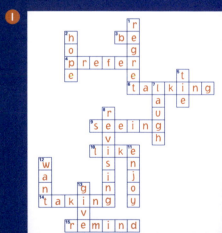

🔧 Fix it notes

A
Use the -ing form (not the infinitive) after a preposition, e.g. in, without.

B
Use the -ing form (not the infinitive) after some verbs, e.g. deny, dislike, love, suggest.

C
Some verbs are followed by the infinitive (not the -ing form), e.g. hope, would prefer.

D
Use the infinitive after regret when it means that you are sorry about something you're going to say. Use the infinitive after stop when it means that you stop doing one thing in order to do another thing.

E
Use the -ing form after remember and forget when you're talking about a memory.

F
Some verbs are followed by object + infinitive, e.g. advise, persuade, teach, want.

G
Use object + base form of the verb after let and make.

For more information, see the Review page opposite. ▷

 Review

Verb patterns

Using the *-ing* form

- You use the *-ing* form (not the infinitive) after a preposition, e.g. *about, at, in, like, of, without,* etc.
  We're really looking forward to seeing you.   *Is Charlie interested in music?*

- You use the *-ing* form (not the infinitive) after some verbs, e.g. *can't bear, can't stand, dislike, don't mind, enjoy, finish, go, hate, like, love, mean, suggest,* etc.
  It means getting up really early but at least the flight is cheap.

  The verb *go* is very common when you're talking about sports.
  I suggested going to Majorca.   *Let's go jogging/swimming/cycling.*

Using the infinitive

- You use the infinitive (not the *-ing* form) after some verbs, e.g. *agree, decide, hope, learn, manage, need, promise, want, would like/love/hate/prefer,* etc.
  She promised not to eat the sweets.   *He'd prefer to pay cash if that's OK.*

Verbs that take both the *-ing* form and infinitive

- You use the *-ing* form or the infinitive after some verbs, e.g. *forget, regret, remember, stop, try.* Be careful! The meaning of the verb changes.
  stop
  Sheila stopped to say hello. (She stopped what she was doing. She said 'Hello'.)
  Mary stopped saying she was hungry. (She kept saying she was hungry. Then she stopped.)
  forget
  I forgot to lock the car. (It's unlocked.)
  I'll never forget meeting you for the first time. (It's an important memory.)
  remember
  Do you remember meeting me for the first time? (Is it a memory you have?)
  Did you remember to lock the car? (Sometimes you forget.)
  regret
  I regret shouting at the dog. (I shouted. I'm sorry that I did.)
  I regret to say you're fired. (I'm going to tell you you're fired. I'm sorry about it.)

Object + infinitive

- You can put the object + infinitive after some verbs, e.g. *advise, allow, encourage, help, order, persuade, prefer, remind, teach, want,* etc.
  We encouraged the children to learn French as well as Italian.

- Be careful! After *let* and *make* you use object + base form of the verb.
  Mum let us watch TV last night. She made us do our homework first though.

Action and state verbs

Test it ✔

① **Choose the best option. If both options are possible, choose both.**

a   Oh, no! Last week I .... 50 kilos. This week it's 56!
   A weighed   **B** was weighing

b   Oonagh .... a letter when I called in to see her.
   A wrote   **B** was writing

c   These kids .... too much noise.
   A make   **B** are making

d   Why on earth .... at me like that? Is there something on my face?
   A do you look   **B** are you looking

e   Billy .... a word his teacher said this morning.
   A wasn't understanding   **B** didn't understand

f   Jo .... a house in Lucca.
   A has   **B** is having

g   Anthony .... amazed when I told him the news.
   A looked   **B** was looking

h   I .... this headline! 'Man bites dog' – it sounds absurd.
   A 'm not believing   **B** don't believe

i   We .... someone to love.
   A are all needing   **B** all need

j   Sarah says she .... a bit sick this morning.
   A feels   **B** 's feeling

② **Write the correct form of the verbs in brackets.**

a   I (know) you love me really.

b   Karen (admire) Richard.

c   Now I (taste) the soup to see if it's got enough salt in it.

d   (you / want) anything or are you OK?

e   The party's great, Mark. We (have) a fantastic time.

f   Natasha (not / mean) to be rude to me yesterday.

g   I (belong) to a bird-watching club and I love it!

h   You look sad. What (you / think) about?

i   The judge (feel) that the appropriate sentence is ten years in jail.

j   Louise (not / understand) what you said.

20

GO to page 76 and check your answers.

Test it again ✔

1 **Complete the dialogues. Use the simple or continuous forms of the verbs. If both forms are possible, write both.**

Kim: What ª .... (you / do)?

Nick: I ᵇ .... (measure) the staircase. We

ᶜ.................................... (need) a new carpet for it.

Boy: Can you come upstairs? My head ᵈ .... (hurt).
I ᵉ .... (think) I'm ill.

Mother: OK. I ᶠ .... (come), don't worry.

ᵍ.................................... (you / want) an aspirin?

Boss: So, Mr Jones, I ʰ .... (understand) you

ⁱ.................................... (not / like) working for us any more. Is that
right?

Employee: Well, yes. I ʲ .... (feel) it's time I changed my
career.

Andy: What ᵏ .... (we / have) for lunch? I'm starving.

Kate: I'm not sure any more. This ham I bought yesterday

ˡ.................................... (taste) a bit funny to me. Here, you try it.

2 **Choose the best option.**

a This can is containing/contains paraffin so be careful with it.
b Hi, Monica. I'm admiring/admire your garden. What's that rose called?
c I'm thinking/think we should go and live somewhere hot. How about you?
d We have/'re having a lovely time in Switzerland. I wish you were here.
e We went to a terrible restaurant. The soup was tasting/tasted like water.
f You seem/are seeming very worried. Is everything OK?
g It really isn't mattering/doesn't matter what I think.
h That motorbike costs/is costing too much. I'll take the other one.
i Poor Debbie. She's feeling/feels she made the wrong decision.
j You strongly resemble/are strongly resembling an old boyfriend of mine.

| 12 |

🔧 Fix it

Answers to Test it

Check your answers. Wrong answer?
Read the right Fix it note to find out why.

1
a	A	→ C	f	A	→ C
b	B	→ A	g	A	→ C
c	A, B	→ A	h	B	→ B
d	B	→ D	i	B	→ B
e	B	→ B	j	A, B	→ E

2
a	know	→ B
b	admires	→ C
c	'm tasting	→ D
d	Do you want	→ B
e	're having	→ D
f	didn't mean	→ B
g	belong	→ B
h	are you thinking	→ D
i	feels	→ C
j	didn't understand	→ B

Now go to page 75. Test yourself again.

Answers to Test it again

1
a	are you doing	g	do you want
b	I'm measuring	h	understand
c	need	i	don't like
d	hurts/is hurting	j	feel
e	think	k	are we having
f	'm coming	l	tastes

2
a	contains	f	seem
b	'm admiring	g	doesn't matter
c	think	h	costs
d	're having	i	feels
e	tasted	j	strongly resemble

🔧 Fix it notes

A
Use action verbs in the simple or continuous form, depending on the situation. Follow the usual rules.

B
Use the simple form (not the continuous) with most state verbs, e.g. *believe, belong, know, mean, need, understand* and *want*.

C
Use the simple form (not the continuous) when certain verbs, e.g. *admire, feel, have, look, weigh*, etc., have stative meanings.

D
Use the continuous form (not the simple) when certain verbs, e.g. *have, look, taste* and *think*, have active meanings.

E
Use the simple or continuous form with a few state verbs, e.g. *feel*, when there's no difference in meaning.

For more information, see the Review page opposite. ▷

 **Review**

Action and state verbs

Verbs can express either states or actions. An action means that something happens. Some typical action verbs are *decide, go, jump, listen, run, speak* and *work.*

A state means that something remains the same. Some typical state verbs are *like, love, hate, know, believe* and *understand.*

You use action and state verbs differently in English. Here are some rules to help you decide whether to use the simple or continuous form with certain verbs.

Action verbs

- You use action verbs in the simple or continuous form, depending on the situation.
  I often go to the cinema.   Where are you going?
  Stan read fifteen books last month.
  Yesterday, I was reading a book by Duncan Forbes.

State verbs

- You use the simple form (not the continuous) with most state verbs.
  This medication contains caffeine. NOT *This medication is containing caffeine.*
  Do you need anything? NOT *Are you needing anything?*

- You use the simple or continuous form with a few state verbs when there is no difference in meaning. These verbs are *feel, ache* and *hurt.*
  I'm feeling a bit depressed. OR *I feel a bit depressed.*
  My head's aching. OR *My head aches.*
  My tummy's hurting. OR *My tummy hurts.*

Note: It's possible that you'll hear native speakers using other state verbs in the continuous form. However, if you want to be sure you don't make mistakes, it's probably best to follow these rules.

State and action verbs

- Some verbs can have both a state and an action meaning. You use the simple form (not the continuous) when they have stative meanings. For some examples, see page 86.

Note: With verbs of perception (*feel, hear, see, smell, taste*) you often use *can/can't* and *could/couldn't.*
I could hear the waves crashing down on the beach.
I can taste curry in this dish.   *Can you smell burning?*
He can't see you!   *She couldn't feel anything.*

Confusing verbs

Test it ✅

1 **Choose the best option.**

a John talks and talks and talks and yet he never says/tells anything.
b I don't like my boss. He makes/lets me do all the photocopying.
c Are you coming/going round to my place this evening?
d Do stop talking/speaking rubbish.
e When you go/come round, could you bring my video back?
f What language do they speak/talk in Uzbekistan?
g Please say/tell me what's wrong.
h Let's begin/start Word and write the letter.
i I'm going to bring/fetch the kids from school now. Back in a sec.
j Oh, please make/let me stay up and watch the film.

2 **Find and correct the mistakes in the verbs in each sentence.**

a Could you please tell that again? I didn't hear you properly.
b Have I ever said you I love you?
c 'Could you come here, please?' 'OK. I'm going.'
d He talks French well.
e I'll make you stay if you promise to be good.
f I can't begin the engine. I think there's something wrong with it.
g Could you fetch this video back to the shop for me?
h Kate's bringing her dog to the vet's. He's unwell.
i Lia said us a joke yesterday. It was very funny.
j I'd love to come and live in Italy but I can't.

20

GO to page 80 and check your answers.

Test it again ✓

1 **Choose the best option.**

a Don't .... me you've lost your keys again.
A say   **B** tell

b French and Flemish are .... in Belgium.
A talked   **B** spoken

c It was a great day. They even .... us stroke the kangaroos.
A made   **B** let

d Why don't you .... round to Jean's place and ask her out?
A go   **B** come

e Shall I .... you out somewhere tonight?
A bring   **B** take

f Can you .... me what the time is, please?
A tell   **B** say

g What complete rubbish you ....
A speak   **B** talk

h 'Where's the corkscrew?' 'In the kitchen. I'll go and .... it.'
A bring   **B** fetch

i Let's .... to the park.
A go   **B** come

j Liz .... the truth. Mark lied.
A said   **B** told

2 **Complete the sentences with a verb from the list in the correct form.**

say   make   fetch   tell   go   come   talk (x2)   speak   start

a I once met a man who just couldn't stop .... lies.

b As soon as term finishes I'm .... to Spain.

c He has travelled a lot and .... several languages.

d He's a good dog. I throw the ball and he .... it.

e I .... Microsoft Windows but nothing happened.

f Let's invite John to the meeting. He always .... sense!

g The baby .... her first word. It was 'dog', unfortunately.

h .... over here. I want to show you something.

i If only animals could .... to us. I wonder what they'd say.

j My mum .... me come home by ten o'clock.

20

Fix it

Answers to Test it

Check your answers. Wrong answer? Read the right Fix it note to find out why.

1
a says	→ A	f speak	→ C
b makes	→ F	g tell	→ B
c coming	→ D	h start	→ G
d talking	→ C	i fetch	→ E
e come	→ D	j let	→ F

2
a ~~tell~~	say	→ A
b ~~said~~	told	→ A, B
c ~~going~~	coming	→ D
d ~~talks~~	speaks	→ C
e ~~make~~	let	→ F
f ~~begin~~	start	→ G
g ~~fetch~~	take	→ E
h ~~bringing~~	taking	→ E
i ~~said~~	told	→ A, B
j ~~come~~	go	→ D

Now go to page 79. Test yourself again.

Answers to Test it again

1
a B	b B	c B	d A	e B
f A	g B	h B	i A	j B

2
a telling	f talks
b going	g said
c speaks	h Come
d fetches	i talk
e started	j makes

Fix it notes

A
Use *say* (not *tell*) to talk about speech in general. Use *tell* (not *say*) when you're informing or instructing someone. Use *tell* in certain fixed expressions with *joke, story, lie,* etc.

B
Put a personal direct object or someone's name after *tell/told*. Don't put a personal direct object after *say/said*.

C
Use *speak* to refer to languages and the physical ability to speak. Use *talk* in expressions with *rubbish, sense,* etc.

D
Use *come* for a movement in the direction of the speaker. Use *go* for a movement away from the speaker.

E
Use *bring* to talk about a movement in the direction of the speaker. Use *take* to talk about other movements. Use *fetch* when you mean 'go and bring back'.

F
Use *make* to force someone to do something. Use *let* to allow someone to do something.

G
Use *start* (not *begin*) when you're setting something in motion, e.g. an engine.

For more information, see the Review page opposite.

 Review

Confusing verbs

Say, speak, tell and *talk*

- You use *say* (not *tell*) to talk about speech in general. You use *tell* (not *say*) when you're informing someone about something or giving them instructions.
  He said something funny the other day.   *What did you say?*
  I told you not to climb on the chairs.   *I'll tell you how to get there.*

- Always put a personal direct object or someone's name after *tell* and *told*. Never put a personal direct object after *say* or *said*.
  We're going to tell Katy about the article.   *Did you say something?*

- You use *tell* in certain fixed expressions.
  Tell lies/a story/the time/a joke/the truth/the difference.

- You use *speak* when you're referring to languages and to refer to the physical ability to speak.
  I speak French and Italian.   *Of course he can't speak to you. He's a rabbit.*

- You use *talk* in fixed expressions with *rubbish, nonsense, sense*, etc. and to refer to the act of speaking.
  Don't talk rubbish.   *Let's talk about it tonight.*   *Come and talk to me!*

Come and *go*; *bring, take* and *fetch*

- You use *come* to talk about a movement in the direction of the speaker or the person you're speaking to. You use *go* to talk about a movement away from the speaker or the person you're speaking to.
  Come over here a second.   *I'd love to go to Venezuela.*

- You use *bring* to talk about a movement in the direction of the speaker or the person you're speaking to. You use *take* to talk about other movements. You use *fetch* when you mean 'go and bring back'.
  Could you bring a bottle of wine round?   *I'll take the laptop with me.*
  My dog's good at fetching sticks.

Make and *let*; *start* and *begin*

- You use *make* when someone forces someone else to do something. You use *let* when someone allows someone else to do something.
  He makes me do the washing-up.   *Will you let me come with you?*

- You use *start* (not *begin*) when you're referring to setting something in motion, e.g. an engine, a computer program. Otherwise there is very little difference in meaning between *start* and *begin*. If you're in doubt, use *start*.
  Let's see if we can start this car.   *I want to start a family.* (= have children)

Phrasal verbs

Test it ✔

1 **Find the incorrect sentences.**

a The milk's gone off. It smells terrible!

b The building is unstable. They're going to knock down it.

c Joey takes his father after. They've got the same eyes.

d I just don't know the answer. I give up.

e Take off your jacket and make yourself comfortable.

f I can't hear the music. Can you please turn up it?

g Have you let the dog out?

h We can't put this situation up with any longer.

i That's strange — Karen's gone off somewhere.

j If you'd like to come and see us, we can put you up for the night.

k How on earth are we going to get this problem round?

2 **Choose the best option.**

a Could you pick up me/pick me up from the office?
b Jason made it up/made up it.
c Natalie went back her promise on/went back on her promise.
d Jim asked you after/asked after you.
e Can you look after my puppy/look my puppy after?

16

GO to page 84 and check your answers.

Test it again ✔

1 **Complete the sentences. Use a phrasal verb from the list in the correct tense.**

run out of	*get over*	*set off*	*tell off*	*let down*
put up	*switch off*	*knock down*	*take off*	*look up*

a Did the plane .... on time?

b He'll never .... his grandmother's death.

c We could .... you .... for the night if you like.

d The teacher .... the children .... for fighting.

e Could you .... the number .... in the telephone directory?

f George has really .... me .... this time. He failed his exams again.

g They're going to .... these flats and build houses.

h Don't tell me we've .... milk again.

i If we don't .... soon, we won't get there in time.

j We don't need that light on. Could you .... it .... ?

2 **Find and correct the mistake in each sentence.**

a He kept working on all night.

b I think I'll go with Charlie out if he asks me.

c You'll feel better when you've got your cold over.

d You shouldn't put with your salary up. It's not enough.

e Can you put up me tonight? I've got nowhere to go.

f How do you manage to get on so little money by?

g The business wasn't doing well so they closed down it.

h Can you get hold some free software of for me?

i Why doesn't he come up a suggestion with?

j She's gone the report through but she can't find the right page.

☐ 20

🔧 Fix it

Answers to Test it

Check your answers. Wrong answer?
Read the right Fix it note to find out why.

1 **a** correct   → **A**
    b ~~knock down it~~
       knock it down   → **B**
    c ~~takes his father after~~
       takes after his father   → **C**
    d correct   → **A**
    e correct   → **B**
    f ~~turn up it~~   turn it up   → **B**
    g correct   → **B**
    h ~~put this situation up with~~
       put up with this situation → **D**
    i correct   → **A**
    j correct   → **B**
    k ~~get this problem round~~
       get round this problem   → **C**

2 **a** pick me up   → **B**
    b made it up   → **B**
    c went back on   → **D**
    d asked after you   → **C**
    e look after my puppy   → **B**

Now go to page 83. Test yourself again.

Answers to Test it again

1 **a** take off   **f** let ... down
    b get over   **g** knock down
    c put ... up   **h** run out of
    d told ... off   **i** set off
    e look ... up   **j** switch ... off

2 **a** kept on working
    b go out with Charlie
    c got over your cold
    d put up with your salary
    e put me up tonight
    f get by on so little
    g closed it down
    h get hold of some
    i come up with a suggestion
    j gone through the report

🔧 Fix it notes

A
Some phrasal verbs don't take an
object. Use subject + phrasal verb.

B
Some phrasal verbs take an object. The
object can go either before or after the
short word (*up, after, in, for,* etc.). If the
object is a pronoun (*me, it, him,* etc.),
put it before the short word.

C
Some phrasal verbs take an object but
you can't put the object between the
verb and the short word (*up, in, after,
for,* etc.).

D
Some phrasal verbs have two short
words (*to, with, forward,* etc.) after the
verb. You can't put the object between
the verb and the short words.

> For more information, see the
> Review page opposite. ▷

 Review

Phrasal verbs

Phrasal verbs are verbs followed by a short word, e.g. *up, in, after*. The short word may be a preposition (*of, for*) or an adverb particle (*away, back*). Phrasal verbs have a meaning that is different from the meaning of the verb itself. So, for example, you may know what the verb *break* means but that doesn't necessarily help you to understand the phrasal verb *break off*. You can learn phrasal verbs in the same way that you learn new items of vocabulary but you also need to know the following rules.

- Some phrasal verbs don't take an object. You use the subject + phrasal verb.
  The plane took off at seven.   *We set off for the beach early that morning.*
  (The plane left the runway.)   (We went to the beach.)

  Note that phrasal verbs can often have more than one meaning.
  This meat has gone off.   *Paddy's gone off somewhere. I don't know where.*
  (It's bad. We can't eat it.)   (Paddy's gone away.)

- Some phrasal verbs take an object. The object can go either before or after the short word. If the object is a pronoun (*me, it, her*, etc.), you put it before the short word.
  *We've **cut** the old apple tree **down**.*   OR   *We've **cut down** the old apple tree.*
  *We've **cut** it **down**.*   NOT   ~~We've cut down it.~~
  *I **picked** Billy **up** at the station.*   OR   *I **picked up** Billy at the station.*
  *I **picked** him **up**.*   NOT   ~~I picked up him.~~

- Some phrasal verbs take an object but you can't put the object between the verb and the short word.
  *Sally **takes after** her mother.*   NOT   ~~Sally takes her mother after.~~
  (She looks or behaves like her mother.)
  *Sally **takes after** her.*   NOT   ~~Sally takes her after.~~

- Some phrasal verbs have two short words after the verb. You can't put the object between the verb and the short words.
  *I'm sorry. We've **run out of** coffee.*   NOT   ~~We've run coffee out of.~~
  (We haven't got any coffee left.)
  *I've **come up with** a brilliant idea!*   NOT   ~~I've come a brilliant idea up with.~~
  (I've had a brilliant idea.)

State and action verbs

State	Action
I **have** (= own) a small house.	I'm **having** lunch/a bath/a great time.
I **think** (= believe) you're right.	What **are** you **thinking** about at the moment?
I **feel** (= have an opinion) it's the right thing to do.	I'm **feeling** a bit depressed.
He **looks** (= seems) happy.	What's the cat **looking** at?
He **appears** (= seems) to be happy.	He's **appearing** on several chat shows today.
I **see** (= understand) the problem.	**Are** you **seeing** the doctor this morning?
I **weigh** about 52 kilos.	I'm just **weighing** the ingredients.
Pete's **measuring** himself. He's growing fast.	The room **measures** 10 metres by 5 metres.
I'm **smelling** the milk to see if it's gone off.	This meat **smells** bad.
She's **tasting** the soup in case it needs more salt.	It **tastes** like water but it's lemonade.
How much **is** it **costing** you to repair the roof?	How much **does** this **cost**?
I'm just **admiring** your car. It looks great.	I really **admire** your courage.
She's **caring** for the sick in Calcutta at the moment.	I don't **care** what you say.

Verb forms

Present forms of verbs

Present simple of *be*
I'm
he/she/it's
we/you/they're
I'm **not**
he/she/it **isn't**
we/you/they **aren't**
Am I?
Is he/she/it?
Are we/you/they?

Present simple
I/we/you/they **work**
he/she/it **works**
I/we/you/they **don't work**
he/she/it **doesn't work**
Do I/we/you/they **work?**
Does he/she/it **work?**

Present continuous
I'm **working**
he/she/it's **working**
we/you/they're **working**
I'm **not working**
he/she/it **isn't working**
we/you/they **aren't working**
Am I **working?**
Is he/she/it **working?**
Are we/you/they **working?**

Past forms of verbs

Past simple of *be*
I/he/she/it **was**
we/you/they **were**
I/he/she/it **wasn't**
we/you/they **weren't**
Was I/he/she/it?
Were we/you/they?

Past simple of regular verbs
I/he/she/it/we/you/they **worked**
I/he/she/it/we/you/they **didn't work**
Did I/he/she/it/you/they **work?**

Past simple of irregular verbs
I/he/she/it/we/you/they **went**
I/he/she/it/we/you/they **didn't go**
Did I/he/she/it/we/you/they **go?**

Past continuous
I/he/she/it **was working**
we/you/they **were working**
I/he/she/it **wasn't working**
we/you/they **weren't working**
Was I/he/she/it **working?**
Were we/you/they working?

Present perfect simple
I/we/you/they've **worked**
he/she/it's **worked**
I/we/you/they **haven't worked**
he/she/it **hasn't worked**
Have I/we/you/they **worked?**
Has he/she/it **worked?**

Present perfect continuous
I/we/you/they've **been working**
he/she/it's **been working**
I/we/you/they **haven't been working**
he/she/it **hasn't been working**
Have I/we/you/they **been working?**
Has he/she/it **been working?**

Past perfect simple
I/he/she/it/we/you/they'd **seen**
I/he/she/it/we/you/they **hadn't seen**
Had I/he/she/it/we/you/they **seen?**

Irregular verbs

Common irregular verbs

Base form	Past simple	Past participle	Base form	Past simple	Past participle
beat	beat	beaten	know	knew	known
become	became	become	learn	learnt	learnt
begin	began	begun	leave	left	left
bend	bent	bent	lend	lent	lent
bite	bit	bitten	light	lit	lit
bleed	bled	bled	lose	lost	lost
blow	blew	blown	make	made	made
break	broke	broken	meet	met	met
bring	brought	brought	pay	paid	paid
build	built	built	put	put	put
burn	burnt	burnt	read	read	read
burst	burst	burst	ride	rode	ridden
buy	bought	bought	ring	rang	rung
catch	caught	caught	run	ran	run
choose	chose	chosen	say	said	said
come	came	come	see	saw	seen
cost	cost	cost	sell	sold	sold
cut	cut	cut	send	sent	sent
deal	dealt	dealt	shake	shook	shaken
dig	dug	dug	shine	shone	shone
do	did	done	shoot	shot	shot
draw	drew	drawn	show	showed	shown
dream	dreamt	dreamt	shut	shut	shut
drink	drank	drunk	sing	sang	sung
drive	drove	driven	sink	sank	sunk
eat	ate	eaten	sit	sat	sat
fall	fell	fallen	sleep	slept	slept
feed	fed	fed	smell	smelt	smelt
feel	felt	felt	speak	spoke	spoken
fight	fought	fought	spell	spelt	spelt
find	found	found	spend	spent	spent
fly	flew	flown	spill	spilt	spilt
forget	forgot	forgotten	stand	stood	stood
forgive	forgave	forgiven	steal	stole	stolen
freeze	froze	frozen	stick	stuck	stuck
get	got	got	swim	swam	swum
give	gave	given	take	took	taken
go	went	gone/been	teach	taught	taught
grow	grew	grown	tear	tore	tore
have	had	had	tell	told	told
hear	heard	heard	think	thought	thought
hide	hid	hidden	throw	threw	thrown
hit	hit	hit	understand	understood	understood
hold	held	held	wear	wore	worn
hurt	hurt	hurt	win	won	won
keep	kept	kept	write	wrote	written